Dining In—Napa Valley
COOKBOOK

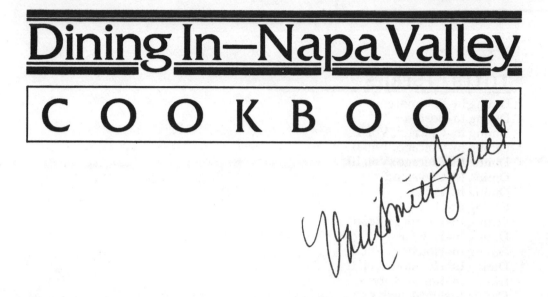

TITLES IN SERIES

Dining In–Baltimore
Dining In–Boston
Dining In–Chicago, Vol. I
Dining In–Chicago, Vol. II
Dining In–Chicago, Vol. III
Dining In–Cleveland
Dining In–Dallas
Dining In–Denver
Dining In–Hampton Roads
Dining In–Hawaii
Dining In–Houston, Vol. I
Dining In–Houston, Vol. II
Dining In–Kansas City
Dining In–Los Angeles
Dining In–Miami
Dining In–Manhattan
Dining In–Milwaukee
Dining In–Minneapolis/St. Paul, Vol. I
Dining In–Minneapolis/St. Paul, Vol. II
Dining In–Monterey Peninsula
Dining In–Napa Valley
Dining In–New Orleans
Dining In–Philadelphia
Dining In–Phoenix
Dining In–Pittsburgh
Dining In–Portland
Dining In–St. Louis
Dining In–Salt Lake City
Dining In–San Francisco, Vol. I
Dining In–San Francisco, Vol. II
Dining In–Seattle, Vol. I
Dining In–Seattle, Vol. II
Dining In–Seattle, Vol. III
Dining In–Sun Valley
Dining In–Toronto
Dining In–Vancouver, B.C.
Dining In–Washington, D.C.

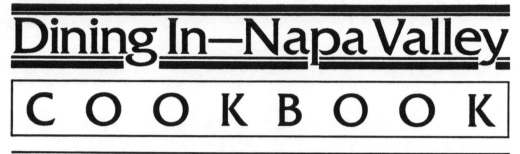

Dining In—Napa Valley

C O O K B O O K

A Collection of Gourmet Recipes for Complete Meals
from Napa Valley's Finest Restaurants

VALLI SMITH FERRELL

Foreword by
ROBERT MONDAVI

Peanut Butter Publishing
Seattle, Washington

Editor: Peggy Mellody
Photography & Design: Christopher Conrad
Styling & Design: Charmaine Eads
Production: Sara L. Jewett, Burke Knouse
Illustration: Margrit Biever
Typesetting: Ricardo Birmele, The Cantilever Group

Foreword 1

Auberge du Soleil 3

La Belle Hélène 13

Bombard's 23

La Boucane 35

Cafe Oriental 43

Calistoga Inn 51

D.D. Kay's Uptown Bar and Grill 59

The Diner 69

Domaine Chandon 79

The French Laundry 87

Mama Nina's 97

Meadowood Resort 107

Miramonte Restaurant and Country Inn 117

Mount View Hotel 127

Mustards Grill 135

St. George Restaurant 145

Silverado Country Club 151

Silverado Restaurant 157

Spring Street Restaurant 165

Swan Court Cafe 173

Venturi's 181

Index 189

FOREWORD

Napa Valley was unknown in the world of wine ten years ago. Today we belong in the company of the fine wines of the world.

We have the natural elements; the climate, the soil, the grape varieties, and we have and are developing the knowledge and know-how to produce outstanding wines. During the last five or six years we have experienced a revolution in the culinary arts which started in our own Bay Area. Just as in wine, we have the natural elements for cooking—the fish, the fowl, the meats, the vegetables, fruits and grains; and we are learning the skills of gastronomy.

I do believe in the next generation our country will become a shining light in wine and food. We are moving with the changing times to more elegant wines; to lighter, fresher, more interesting foods and food preparation. Both of these trends are healthier and more palatable.

It is only fitting and proper that out of Napa Valley a book revealing some of the recipes of our fine restaurants should be published.

Robert Mondavi
Oakville, California

Dinner for Four

Fricassée of Wild Mushrooms
Sauce Perigueux

Partridge with Two Purées and Purple Basil Fumé

Spring Salad

Passion Fruit Cheesecake

WINES:

With the Mushrooms—Rutherford Hill Merlot, 1980

With the Partridge—Cakebread Sauvignon Blanc, 1984

With the Cheesecake—S. Anderson Blanc de Noirs

Claude Rouas, Owner

Michel Cornu, Chef

Nestled in a thirty-three acre olive grove on the Eastern hillside above Rutherford rises the prestigious Auberge du Soleil. Spectacular views of the patchwork valley floor and surrounding mountains capture the serene beauty of the Napa Valley. The Auberge du Soleil, an elegant French-style country inn, sits here in stately harmony with its surroundings.

Claude Rouas, charming proprietor of the Auberge du Soleil and also of the famous L'Etoile Restaurant in San Francisco, came to the Napa Valley twelve years ago searching for a spot for a small country inn. He found the perfect spot, and in 1981 opened a restaurant which quickly won the high acclaim of food critics nationwide and assumed a key position on the culinary map.

Since then, the restaurant has blossomed into a luxurious resort, with the nearby addition of thirty-six rooms and nine private "maisons", all richly and tastefully appointed. Guests may relax poolside or enjoy a set of tennis before leisurely walking up the hill for a dinner they will not soon forget.

The restaurant is still the resort's most prized feature. Says Claude, "I believe the Napa Valley will in a few years become to the U.S. what Burgundy is to France, the culinary center of the country."

Taking that lead is Auberge du Soleil's French chef, Michel Cornu. Cornu uses in his cooking what he calls the "richesse de la terroir", or an abundance of fine, fresh local products. He creates classic French dishes with a nouvelle flair, concentrating on light and beautiful presentations.

180 Rutherford Hill Road
Rutherford

FRICASSEE OF WILD MUSHROOMS
SAUCE PERIGUEUX

½ cup butter	1 teaspoon chopped garlic
4 ounces porcini mushrooms, sliced	1 teaspoon chopped parsley
4 ounces shiitake mushrooms, sliced	1 teaspoon chopped chives
4 ounces oyster mushrooms, sliced	2 duck legs, confit*
4 ounces chanterelles, sliced	Salt and pepper

1. Melt butter in a skillet over high heat and sauté porcini mushrooms, shiitake mushrooms, oyster mushrooms, and chanterelles until cooked, about 4 to 5 minutes. Season to taste with salt and pepper. Add garlic, parsley, and chives. Sauté for two minutes.

2. Add duck legs. Toss with mushrooms, and heat gently for 2 to 3 minutes.

3. Remove meat from bones and add meat to mushrooms. Serve immediately with SAUCE PERIGUEUX.

4. To serve, place mushrooms in center of individual serving plates. Carefully ladle SAUCE PERIGUEUX around mushrooms. Serve immediately.

Duck confit is duck that has been poached and preserved in duck fat. A substitute for the confit might be a 4 ounce tin of duck liver, cut into pieces and sautéed at the last minute with the mushrooms.

SAUCE PERIGUEUX

2 teaspoons chopped shallots
2 tablespoons butter
2 cups Madeira
½ cup port wine
    Pinch of cracked black pepper

2 cups veal demi-glace*
2 ounces truffle peelings*
2 tablespoons truffle juice*
2 bay leaves

1. Sweat shallots in butter in a saucepan over low heat. Add Madeira, port, bay leaves, and a pinch of cracked black pepper. Increase heat to high and reduce to one-third of original volume.

2. Add veal demi-glace and reduce for ten minutes. Strain sauce.

3. Blend in truffle peeling and truffle juice. Season to taste.

* May be purchased in gourmet food stores.

PARTRIDGE WITH TWO PUREES
AND PURPLE BASIL FUME

1 pound peas	*3 tablespoons heavy (whipping) cream*
4 cups chicken stock	*2 ears young white corn*
¼ cup sherry	*4 18-ounce partridges*
½ cup plus 2 tablespoons butter	*2 tablespoons Armagnac*
Salt and white pepper to taste	*PURPLE BASIL FUME*

1. Simmer peas in 2 cups of stock and the sherry in a saucepan for 5 minutes. Drain peas, reserving ¼ cup peas for garnish. Place remaining peas in a blender with 2 tablespoons butter and heavy cream. Purée until smooth. Season with salt and pepper. Set aside and keep warm.

2. Cut corn from cob and simmer with remaining 2 cups of stock in a saucepan for 5 minutes. Drain corn; reserving ¼ cup for garnish. Place remaining corn in a blender with 2 tablespoons butter. Purée until smooth. Season with salt and pepper. Set aside and keep warm while preparing partridges.

3. Preheat oven to 375 degrees. Season partridges with salt and pepper. Melt remaining butter in a large ovenproof skillet over medium high heat and sauté partridges, browning on all sides. Pour Armagnac over partridges. Bake partridges in skillet until medium-rare, about 10 minutes, or until fork inserted in center causes juices to run slightly pink.

4. Remove partridges from pan and remove legs, de-boning thigh bone. Remove both breasts, cutting close to the breastbone. Reserve carcasses for Purple Basil Fumé. Set legs and breasts aside and prepare Purple Basil Fumé.

5. To serve, reheat breasts and legs in oven with a little wine until warm. Remove and slice breasts, fanlike, keeping meat joined at one end. Place enough Purple Basil Fumé to cover the bottom of warm individual serving plates. Place two separate beds of pea purée and corn purée over the Fumé. Top each serving with a fanned breast. Place two legs artfully onto the Fumé on either side of the breast. Garnish with reserved peas, corn, and fresh basil leaves. Serve immediately.

PURPLE BASIL FUME

½ large onion, chopped
¼ plus 2 tablespoons butter
  Pinch of cracked pepper
2 bay leaves
4 partridge carcasses

½ cup white wine
1 cup heavy (whipping) cream
5 tablespoons chopped purple basil
8 basil leaves, for garnish

1. Sauté onion in butter with a pinch of cracked black pepper and bay leaves in a large skillet over medium heat. Do not brown. Increase heat to medium-high. Add partridge carcasses and brown on all sides.

2. Decrease heat to low. Add white wine and reduce to one-third its volume.

3. Increase heat to high. Add heavy cream and reduce until sauce is thick enough to coat the back of a spoon.

4. Strain sauce through a fine sieve, pressing hard on solids.

5. Combine strained sauce and chopped basil in a blender. Blend until basil is reduced to tiny flecks. If necessary, reheat gently.

SPRING SALAD

1 head rocket lettuce
Mâche for 4 salads
VINAIGRETTE

1 head Belgian endive
1 head radiccio, julienned

1. Separate, wash, and dry greens.

2. Place into a salad bowl and toss gently with VINAIGRETTE.

VINAIGRETTE

1½ tablespoons Balsamic vinegar
1 teaspoon minced cilantro
2 tablespoons hazelnut oil

2 tablespoons peanut oil
salt and pepper to taste
1 teaspoon minced shallots

1. Blend together vinegar, salt and pepper, shallots, and cilantro in a small bowl with a mixer or a whisk for 2 minutes. Slowly add hazelnut oil and peanut oil, whisking constantly. Season to taste.

PASSION FRUIT CHEESE CAKE

Unsalted butter,
for greasing pan
6-8 graham crackers,
crushed
1 scant cup sugar
3 tablespoons corn starch
3 eggs
½ cup plus 2 tablespoons sour cream
3 8-ounce packages cream cheese, softened

½ cup plus 2 tablespoons milk
9 ounces passion fruit purée*
¼ ounce passion fruit extract*
2 tablespoons Myers's rum
Blackberry or strawberry sorbet,
for garnish
Candied violets, for garnish

1. Butter a 10-inch springform pan. Dust sides and bottom with graham cracker crumbs. (This should be a very thin layer, leaving only the crumbs that stick to the butter.) Set aside.

2. Preheat oven to 325 degrees. Blend cream cheese in a large mixing bowl until smooth. Sift sugar and cornstarch into cream cheese, blending until smooth. Add eggs one at a time, blending well after each addition. Blend in sour cream and milk. Set aside.

3. Mix together passion fruit purée, passion fruit extract, and rum in a medium bowl. Add passion fruit mixture to cream cheese; blend well.

4. Pour filling into prepared pan. Bake for 1½ hours. Remove cheesecake from oven. Cool cheesecake on wire rack; do not remove metal ring. Chill for 4 hours or overnight.

To assemble, remove metal ring from springform pan. Serve cheesecake with a small scoop of blackberry or strawberry sorbet on the side, if desired. Garnish with a candied violet.

*Passion fruit extract can be purchased from gourmet food stores. Pineapple purée can be substituted for the Passion fruit if desired.

Marc Dullin

La Belle Hélène
RESTAURANT

*Unpretentious Elegance
in Dining*

Dinner for Four

*Les Escargots aux Champignons Sauvages
Beurre de Tomate et Basilic*

Fricassée De Faisan au Cabernet Sauvignon

Feuilleté de Poire Caramelisée

WINES:

With the Escargot—Rombauer Chardonnay, 1983

With the Pheasant—Cain Cellars Cabernet Sauvignon, 1982

With the Pears—Raymond Late Harvest Riesling, 1979

Marc Dullin, Owner and Chef

La Belle Hélène Restaurant makes its home in one of Napa Valley's most beautiful stone buildings, the 100-year old "Hatchery", so named because it served as a chicken hatchery for more than 50 years. The Hatchery was placed on the National Register of Historic Places in 1982.

The provincial charm and elegance of the stone exterior is carried through in the restaurant's two dining rooms. Rustic stone walls, country French armoires, and floor-to-ceiling windows that push open onto the street combine to create a serenely beautiful setting that one would expect to find in the French countryside.

Presiding in the kitchen is owner and chef, Marc Dullin, an energetic and straightforward Frenchman who describes his cuisine as "Classic French". His menu includes appetizers such as Fresh Seafood Terrine with Herb Sauce, Escargots with Wild Mushrooms in Puff Pastry, and Duck Pâté with Pistachios and Cumberland Sauce. Delicious entrées like Fresh Norwegian Salmon with Scallop Mousseline and Roast Rack of Lamb with Honey-Thyme Sauce are other examples of his style. Marc creates several special additions to the menu each evening that reflect the season and his choice at market.

La Belle Hélène Restaurant serves only dinner, but may be reserved for private functions.

1345 Railroad Avenue
St. Helena

LA BELLE HELENE RESTAURANT

LES ESCARGOTS AUX CHAMPIGNONS SAUVAGES
BEURRE DE TOMATES ET BASILIC
Snails with Wild Mushrooms
Tomato Basil Butter

4 ounces chanterelles* preferably fresh	½ teaspoon sugar
	Salt to taste
4 ounces cêpe mushrooms,* preferably fresh	½ cup white wine
	½ cup heavy (whipping) cream
1 ripe tomato	6-8 leaves of fresh basil
2 tablespoons unsalted butter	1 cup salted butter, cut into small pieces
2 shallots, finely minced	
1 clove of garlic, pressed	24 Burgundy snails
1 sprig of thyme	2 tablespoons Pernod liqueur
1 bay leaf	Salt and fresh black pepper
3 whole white peppercorns	to taste

1. Wash, dry, and quarter chanterelle and cêpe mushrooms.

2. Bring one quart of salted water to a boil. Meanwhile, make a small "x" on the top of the tomato and remove the core. Plunge the tomato into the boiling water for 15 seconds; remove and plunge into cold water. Peel the tomato. Cut tomato in half, and gently press each half with hands to remove excess water and seeds. Dice tomato into small pieces.

3. Melt 1 tablespoon unsalted butter in a saucepan over medium heat. Add one minced shallot, garlic, thyme, bay leaf, and peppercorns; cooking until shallot is transluscent. Add diced tomato, sugar, and salt; cook for 10 minutes.

4. Add wine to tomato mixture; reduce by one-half. Add heavy cream and bring mixture to a boil. Add basil. Reduce sauce for 5 minutes.

5. Whisk salted butter, one piece at a time, into sauce until butter has melted. Pour sauce into a blender; blend until smooth. Strain sauce through a fine sieve into a bowl. Set aside.

6. Combine 1 tablespoon unsalted butter, remaining shallot, and mushrooms in a sauté pan over high heat.

7. Reduce heat to medium and add snails. Simmer for 5 minutes. Season with salt and pepper.

8. Flame snail mixture with Pernod. Add butter sauce to snail mixture; blend well. Bring mixture to a boil. Serve immediately.

9. Serve on four warm plates, dividing mushrooms and snails evenly among them.

Shiitake or white button mushrooms can be substituted for the wild mushrooms.

FRICASSEE DE FAISAN AU CABERNET SAUVIGNON
Fricassée of Fresh Pheasant in Cain's Cabernet Jelly

1 whole fresh pheasant, quartered	½ bottle Cain Cabernet Sauvignon
1 carrot, chopped coarsely	Salt and freshly ground pepper
2 shallots, minced	1 tablespoon oil
6 whole black peppercorns	2 teaspoons butter
2 whole juniper berries	1 cup strong chicken or veal stock
2 whole cloves garlic	1 cup heavy cream
1 white onion, chopped coarsely	4 ounces Cain's cabernet jelly*
1 bay leaf	½ teaspoon thyme leaves

1. Place pheasant quarters in a large container.

2. Combine carrot, shallots, peppercorns, juniper berries, garlic, onion, bay leaf, thyme, and Cabernet in a bowl. Pour mixture over pheasant. Marinate pheasant overnight.

3. Remove pheasant from marinade and drain by placing it on paper towels. Reserve remaining marinade, separating solids from wine. Salt and pepper both sides of pheasant pieces.

4. Preheat oven to 375 degrees. Heat oil in an oven-proof skillet until hot. Sear pheasant quarters on both sides. Remove pheasant from skillet and discard all fat from skillet.

5. Add butter and marinade solids to skillet over low heat, cooking until vegetables are translucent. Add wine and bring mixture to a boil. Add pheasant quarters and place skillet in oven. Bake for 20 minutes. Remove breasts. Bake legs for an additional 5 to 10 minutes. Keep breasts and legs warm.

6. Return skillet to low heat and reduce sauce to one-quarter of its volume. Add heavy cream and reduce by one-half.

7. Strain sauce through a fine sieve into saucepan over medium heat. Add Cabernet jelly, stirring until jelly is dissolved. Do not boil.

8. To serve, pour sauce onto the four dinner plates. Arrange pheasant on sauce.

* Cain's Cabernet Jelly is produced by Cain Cellars of the Napa Valley. If unavailable at your local gourmet shop, substitute red Currant jelly.

FEUILLETE DE POIRE CARAMELISEE
Caramelized Pears with Creme Anglaise

CREME ANGLAISE

2 cups milk
⅔ cup sugar
½ vanilla bean,
   split lengthwise

4 egg yolks,
   at room temperature
   and beaten slightly

1. Bring milk, sugar, and vanilla to a boil in a heavy saucepan. Remove from heat. Remove vanilla bean.

2. Meanwhile, beat egg yolks in a mixing bowl with a whisk until they are pale yellow.

3. Slowly pour hot milk mixture into eggs, whisking constantly. When milk is incorporated, pour mixture back into saucepan over medium heat; stirring slowly with a wooden spoon until mixture coats the spoon. Do not let mixture come near simmer. Strain sauce through a fine sieve. Set aside.

The Crème Anglaise may be made a day in advance of using; however it will thicken. Thin with a little milk if necessary.

POACHING THE PEARS

2 cups water
1 cup white wine
1 cup sugar
1 whole clove
1 orange, quartered

1 lemon, quartered
1 vanilla bean, cut lengthwise
4 whole black peppercorns
1 bay leaf
2 firm pears

1. Combine water, wine, sugar, clove, orange, lemon, vanilla bean, peppercorns, and bayleaf in a large saucepan over medium-high heat. Bring to a boil and cook for 15 minutes.

2. Meanwhile, peel pears, cut them in half lengthwise and core them. Try to keep the stem on, cutting through stem so that each pear half retains half of the split stem. Plunge pears into boiling syrup and cook for 15 minutes, or until tender. Remove pears from syrup; set aside. Discard syrup or save for another use.*

*The poaching liquid can be strained, reduced it a bit, and then used to moisten cake or to flavor a fruit salad.

CARAMEL

1 cup sugar   ½ cup water

1. Bring sugar and water to a boil in a small heavy saucepan over medium-high heat until sugar turns a caramel color. Cool.

2. Combine caramel with one-half of prepared CREME ANGLAISE; set aside. (Reserve remaining CREME ANGLAISE.)

PUFF PASTRY

1 square puff pastry*   1 egg, beaten

1. Preheat oven to 375 degrees. With a rolling pin roll out puff pastry. Cut dough into 4 3x4-inch rectangles. Place pastry on a baking sheet. Brush top of pastry with beaten egg. Bake for 20 to 25 minutes, or until golden. Cool completely.

2. Split cooled pastry horizontally to make 2 3x4-inch pieces.

*Puff Pastry can be purchased from the bakery or in the frozen food section of the supermarket.

To assemble Feuilleté De Poire Caramelisée:

1. Carefully slice each pear half lengthwise, creating a fan and taking care to keep pear attached at stem. Sprinkle pears with sugar. Place pears under broiler until pears caramelize. Watch carefully, pears burn easily.

2. Spoon caramel mixture on half of the bottoms of 4 dessert plates. Spoon reserved CREME ANGLAISE on other half of plate. Place bottom piece of pastry on top of sauces. Place caramelized pear on top of pastry. Place top piece of pastry slightly to the side of pear.

3. Garnish with a small swirl of whipped cream and a candied violet or a few fresh berries, if desired. Serve immediately after caramelizing pears.

BOMBARDS

Dinner for Six

Andouille Pig Tails

Sooey Salad

File Gumbo

Skillet Cracklin Cornbread

Red Beans

Rice

Grapefruit and Oranges with Bourbon Creme

Pecan Pie

WINES:

With Pig Tails—Joseph Phelps Gewurztraminer

With Sooey Salad—Sterling Sauvignon Blanc

With File Gumbo—Newton Merlot

With Pecan Pie—Beaulieu Muscat de Frontigann

Stephen L. Baldwin, Owner

Joan Baldwin, Chef

Aside from the palate-pleasing Cajun-Creole cuisine at Bombard's, is the eye-pleasing decor. In what would otherwise be a rather ordinary dining room, are two wall-sized murals painted by L.A. artist, Gonzalo Duran, that literally bring the restaurant to life with color and whimsy. One mural, unofficially titled "Life, Love, and Reflection", depicts Chef Joan Baldwin as a young woman and her children all costumed as though whisked in time from Renoir's France. The other mural, equally colorful, is appropriately called "Night in New Orleans". Both murals are reflected in subtle, dark mirrored glass so that diners feel surrounded by the fantasy, quite an appropriate backdrop for what comes out of the kitchen.

Thanks to Chef Joan Baldwin's expert and experienced hand, the Cajun-Creole dishes that are served reflect a perfect balance between delicacy and spiciness. Dishes like Shrimp Remoulade, Oysters Bayou, File Gumbo, and Rabbit Tenderloin in Mustard Sauce are wonderful examples of Joan's cooking.

To know Joan is to know her cooking, for she herself is a colorful and sometimes spicy character. Often seen in the dining room of Bombard's, Joan loves to share bits of folklore with her patrons about Cajun-Creole food and its evolution. She has endeared herself to many with her expansive style. "We are evolving in the restaurant and our next menu will be a little more adventurous. I've tried to bring our clients along, educating their palates to this type of cooking."

Joan spent many childhood years in New Orleans, though she hails from Atlanta. Many of her recipes were handed down through the family, a family that loved to cook and dine well. If there is one thing she believes in strongly, it is that "There are no hard and fast rules to Cajun cooking. You must rely on feeling, instinct and intuition. If you don't have a feeling for the cuisine, you can't do it." For those of us who would like to benefit from the feel that Joan has for Cajun-Creole cooking, try the menu that follows. The recipe for File Gumbo is a family recipe.

4050 Byway East
Napa

ANDOUILLE PIG TAILS

CRUST

One recipe pie crust, see page 32

1. Prepare pie crust.

2. Using a well-floured rolling pin, evenly roll dough into a large 14x10-inch rectangle.

3. Cut crust into 5x2-inch rectangles. Set aside at room temperature.

BAYOU PASTE

¼ pound mushrooms	¼ teaspoon nutmeg
2-3 garlic cloves	¼ teaspoon salt
1 bunch parsley	¼ teaspoon cayenne pepper
1 cup butter, at room temperature	½ pound andouille sausage
1 cup fine bread crumbs	Jalapeno Pepper Jelly, for garnish

1. Combine mushrooms, garlic, and parsley in a food processor; blend well. Add butter. Blend until smooth and creamy. Add bread crumbs, nutmeg, salt, and pepper. Blend until smooth. Set aside.

2. Poach sausage in sauce pan of simmering water for 12 minutes. Remove from heat; cool. Cut sausage lengthwise into 4x⅛-inch strips.

3. Place a rack on a baking sheet. Preheat oven to 375 degrees. Spread a thin layer of BAYOU PASTE over pastry rectangles to within 1-inch of edges. Place a piece of sausage over paste and roll pastry into long cylinders, jelly roll fashion. Pinch edges to make an even seam. Twist both ends like a pigtail. Place pigtails on rack in baking sheet.

4. Bake for 8 to 10 minutes, or until lightly browned.

5. Serve hot or cold with Jalapeno Pepper Jelly, if desired.

Pepper jelly can be purchased in most specialty stores.

SOOEY SALAD

1 pound andouille sausage
1 onion, peeled and left whole
1 1-inch square fresh salt pork
2 cups dry black-eyed peas
½ cup finely minced parsley
½ cup finely minced green onion
½ cup coarsely minced celery
¼ cup coarsely minced red pepper
¼ cup coarsely minced green pepper

1 fresh cayenne pepper,
  finely minced with gloves on
  (or any fresh hot pepper)
Salt to taste
2 red ripe tomatoes,
  cut into wedges
1 large bunch fresh
  tender mustard greens

1. Poach sausage in simmering water for 12 minutes. Remove sausage from water: cool. Thinly slice sausage. Set aside.

2. Add whole onion and salt pork to 10 cups of water in a stock pot. Rinse black-eyed peas in very hot water; drain and add to stock pot. Boil mixture until al dente, about 1 hour. Drain in colander; remove onion and salt pork. Gently rinse black-eyed peas; drain thoroughly.

3. Combine parsley, green onions, celery, red peppers, green peppers, and cayenne pepper. Add beans; toss gently. Season with salt if necessary.

DRESSING

1 cup walnut oil
½ cup white wine vinegar
½ cup coarse brown mustard

⅓ cup club soda
½ teaspoon white pepper
¼ cup brandy, if desired

1. Whisk walnut oil, vinegar, mustard, club soda, pepper, and brandy in a bowl. Reserve ½ cup of dressing.

2. Add remainder to black-eyed pea mixture. Cover and refrigerate for 6 to 8 hours, tossing gently 3 to 4 times during the marinating process.

3. To assemble, carefully wash and towel dry mustard greens; chill. Place greens on chilled salad plates. Using a slotted spoon, arrange black-eyed pea mixture in center of plate. Tuck tomato wedges and sausage slices in among greens. Drizzle reserved dressing over top.

FILE GUMBO
SEAFOOD, FISH, SAUSAGE, CHICKEN, AND HAM

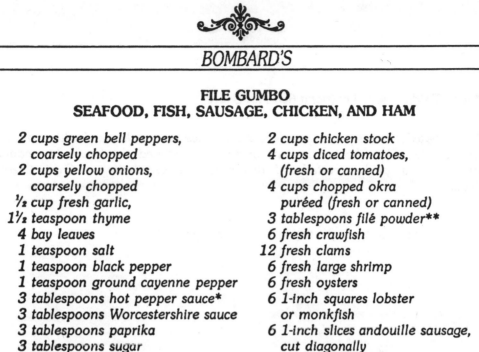

2 cups green bell peppers,
* coarsely chopped*
2 cups yellow onions,
* coarsely chopped*
½ cup fresh garlic,
1½ teaspoon thyme
4 bay leaves
1 teaspoon salt
1 teaspoon black pepper
1 teaspoon ground cayenne pepper
3 tablespoons hot pepper sauce*
3 tablespoons Worcestershire sauce
3 tablespoons paprika
3 tablespoons sugar
1 cup tomato purée
6 cups fish stock

2 cups chicken stock
4 cups diced tomatoes,
* (fresh or canned)*
4 cups chopped okra
* puréed (fresh or canned)*
3 tablespoons filé powder**
6 fresh crawfish
12 fresh clams
6 fresh large shrimp
6 fresh oysters
6 1-inch squares lobster
* or monkfish*
6 1-inch slices andouille sausage,
* cut diagonally*
6 1½-inch rectangles ham
6 1½-inch rectangles chicken

1. Dry sauté (no oil) green peppers and onions in an 8-quart stainless steel stockpot over medium-low heat. Do not use an iron pot or it will turn the okra black. When the vegetables have begun to render their juices and their surfaces appear just caramelized, add garlic; stir.

2. Add thyme, bay leaves, salt, black pepper, cayenne pepper, hot pepper sauce, Worcestershire sauce, paprika and sugar; stir to mix.

3. Mix in tomato purée. Simmer for 5 minutes.

4. Add fish stock and chicken stock; stir well. Simmer for 10 minutes.

5. Add tomatoes and okra; stir gently. Simmer for 20 minutes.

6. Blend filé powder with enough cold water to dissolve it, stirring until smooth. Add filé to gumbo, stirring until completely incorporated. Remove gumbo from heat. Let stand at room temperature for 4 hours.

7. To serve, reheat gumbo to a simmering boil. Add crawfish, clams, shrimp, oysters, lobster, sausage, ham, and chicken; simmer for 20 minutes. Discard any shellfish that does not open. Ladle gumbo into 6 large heated bowls, evenly dividing the seafood and meat. Serve with SKILLET CRACKLIN' CORNBREAD, RED BEANS and RICE. Accompany with GRAPEFRUIT AND ORANGES WITH BOURBON CREME, which will cool the heat from the spicy gumbo!

*Joan Baldwin uses Louisiana Red Hot Sauce.

**Filé powder is dried sassafras leaves that have been pulverized with a mortar and pestle. The Choctaw Indians originally powdered the leaves in wooden mortars, and can be credited with this important contribution to Cajun Creole food.

The gumbo can be made the day before and refrigerated.

SKILLET CRACKLIN' CORNBREAD

2 cups cornmeal
½ cup corn flour
⅓ cup sugar, (optional)
½ teaspoon salt
5 teaspoon baking powder
1⅓ cups buttermilk

5 tablesp. unsalted butter, melted
2 eggs, beaten
½ cup cracklins, finely chopped*
⅔ cup chopped green onions
Vegetable oil

1. Preheat oven to 375 degrees. Stir together cornmeal, corn flour, sugar, baking powder, and salt in a large bowl. Blend together buttermilk, butter, and beaten eggs in a bowl. Mix liquid ingredients into dry ingredients, stirring until just moistened. Fold in green onions and cracklins.

2. Generously oil 6 individual or 1 large cast iron skillet. Heat prepared skillet(s) until very hot. Remove skillet(s) and fill just under ½-full with cornbread batter. The batter should sizzle when it hits the skillet(s). Bake 20 to 25 minutes, or until toothpick inserted in center comes out almost clean.

Preheating the skillets insures a crisp outer crust.

Bombard's makes their own cracklins from pork fat, but you may wish to buy pork skins.

RED BEANS

2 cups dry red beans
10 cups water
1 onion, peeled and left whole

1 1-inch square salt pork
Salt

1. Rinse beans in very hot water; drain.

2. Place water, onion, and salt pork in an 8-quart stock pot. Add beans to pot. Gently simmer mixture until tender and slightly creamy; about 1 hour. Season with salt if necessary.

RICE

3 cups rich chicken stock
2 cups converted long grain rice
  uncooked
1½ tablespoons butter

½ teaspoon salt
Pinch of cayenne pepper
Pinch of garlic powder

1. Bring chicken stock to a boil in a heavy saucepan.

2. Meanwhile, in a saucepan of boiling water, blanch rice to remove outer starchy coating drain. Add rice, butter, salt, pepper, and garlic powder to boiling stock. Reduce heat to low, cover, and steam until no liquid remains and rice is tender, about 20 minutes. Fluff rice with a fork. Serve immediately.

GRAPEFRUIT AND ORANGES WITH BOURBON CREME

3 ruby red grapefruits
4 naval oranges
1 cup heavy (whipping) cream

2 tablespoons Triple Sec
6 tablespoons Bourbon

1. Peel grapefruit and oranges. Remove the sections whole, with no membrane attached. Place segments in a bowl and chill in freezer until icy crystals begin to form. Transfer to refrigerator until ready to serve.

2. Beat whipping cream in a chilled bowl with chilled beaters until soft peaks form. Fold in Triple Sec and Bourbon.

3. To serve, place fruit in a glass serving bowl and top with 3/4 cup BOURBON CREME.

This accompaniment to FILE GUMBO may be served from one large bowl, community-style, or in individual glass dishes.

PECAN PIE

CRUST

1¼ cups all-purpose flour
¼ tablespoon salt
Dash of sugar

½ cup unsalted butter
¼ cup vegetable shortening
3-4 tablespoons ice water

1. Preheat oven to 375 degrees. Sift together flour, salt, and sugar in a bowl. Cut in butter and shortening with a pastry blender or two knives used scissor fashion until mixture resembles coarse crumbs. Sprinkle 1 tablespoon of ice water over mixture; gently toss with a fork. Repeat procedure, blending until mixture is just moistened. With hands, form dough into a ball. Wrap in plastic and chill for 30 minutes.

2. Slightly flatten ball with hands on a lightly floured surface. Using a well-floured rolling pin, evenly roll dough from center to edges into a circle approximately 12 inches in diameter and ⅛-inch thick. Gently transfer dough into pie plate. Trim dough to ½-inch beyond edge of pie plate. Flute edges of dough. Prick shell ½-inches apart over bottom and sides with a fork. Bake for 12 minutes. Cool completely.

Baking the pie crust slightly before filling it helps insure a dry, flaky bottom crust. Baking the filled pie briefly before topping with pecan halves gives the filling a chance to caramelize and gel so that pecan halves do not sink or become overbaked.

FILLING

1 cup chopped unsalted pecans
3 tablespoons butter
¾ cup sugar
2 tablespoons molasses
2 tablespoons honey
1 teaspoons vanilla
3 eggs

¾ cup dark corn syrup
½ teaspoon salt
1 cup unsalted pecan halves,
  whipped cream
  or vanilla ice cream,
  for garnish

1. Preheat oven to 375 degrees. Combine chopped pecans and butter in a large bowl. Gradually add sugar, molasses, honey, and vanilla, stirring constantly. Gradually stir in beaten eggs. Stir in corn syrup and salt. Pour mixture into baked pie shell.

2. Bake for 12 minutes. Remove from oven.

3. Reduce heat to 350 degrees. Arrange pecan halves on top of pie. Bake for 30 minutes.

4. Cool on a wire rack. Serve warm or cool with whipped cream or ice cream if desired.

Dinner for Four

Macedoine California

Cream of Mushroom Soup à la Jacques

Poached Salmon with Champagne Sauce

Strawberries Martine

WINE:

Quail Ridge Chardonnay, 1983

or

Pine Ridge Estate Bottled Chardonnay, 1983

Jacques Mokrani, Owner and Chef

La Boucane is located in a charming old Victorian home. Its dining room and salon are furnished in Period decor and subtly evoke the elegance of another era. "My restaurant is the customer's domain," says Jacques Mokrani, a tall distinguished Algerian who is the owner and chef. He is dedicated to assuring his dinner guests the finest in cuisine and gracious service.

The menu is French and offers such classics as Coquille St. Jacques, Caneton Rôti à L'Orange, and Tournedos Forestière. Desserts offered are equally classic: Mousse Au Chocolat and Crème Caramel. What sets La Boucane apart from being "just another French restaurant" is the execution of the cuisine. Mokrani's Crisp Roast Long Island Duckling is exactly that, crisp and perfectly cooked. The silky texture of his Crème Caramel is yet another testament to his skill. In addition to the menu are daily specials that are created to take advantage of the vast selection of seasonal produce, game, and seafood.

Chef Mokrani is outspoken about his cooking and his restaurant. "There is only one way to do something. It's to do it the right way. There are no shortcuts without sacrificing the taste and the consistency of food."

1778 2nd Street
Napa, California

MACEDOINE CALIFORNIA

1 large or 2 small ripe avocados,
  peeled and diced
4 ounces fresh mushrooms, diced
2 medium size, ripe tomatoes,
  cored and diced
1 teaspoon finely diced onion
  Salt and pepper to taste

4 teaspoons red wine vinegar
2-4 tablespoons good quality
  olive oil*
4 leaves Butter lettuce
4 walnut halves
1 tablespoon chopped parsley

1. Combine avocados, mushrooms, tomatoes, and onion in a salad bowl. Salt and pepper to taste. Sprinkle vinegar over mixture. Add olive oil and toss gently with a wooden spoon or hands.

2. Place one leaf Butter lettuce on each of 4 salad plates. Arrange salad on top. Garnish with one walnut half and parsley.

Macedoine California is Jacques' own creation and somewhat of a trademark for him. A favorite choice of La Boucane patrons, this refreshing salad is served with homemade Whole Wheat Walnut Bread.

*Jacques recommends olive oil from the St. Helena Olive Oil Manufacturing Company.

CREAM OF MUSHROOM SOUP A LA JACQUES

¾ pound fresh white mushrooms
1 medium onion
3 tablespoons unsalted butter
3 cups water

2 Knorr Swiss beef bouillon cubes
2 tablespoons all-purpose flour
1 cup heavy (whipping) cream*
Freshly ground white pepper

1. Grind mushrooms and onions in a food processor or meat grinder.

2. Melt 1 tablespoon butter in a large saucepan over medium-high heat. Add mushroom mixture and cook, stirring constantly, until all water evaporates. Add water and bouillon cubes to mushroom mixture; boil soup for 10 minutes.

3. Meanwhile, combine flour and remaining 2 tablespoons butter until a paste forms (Beurre Manié). Whisk Beurre Manié into soup, whisking until soup thickens.

4. Add heavy cream to soup and bring it to a boil. Skim the top as the soup boils. Season soup heavily with white pepper.

5. Serve soup in bowls accompanied by crusty French bread.

*½ cup whole milk and ½ cup cream can be substituted for the 1 cup cream.

LA BOUCANE

SALMON POACHED WITH CHAMPAGNE SAUCE

1 rounded teaspoon butter,
  at room temperature
1 teaspoon chopped shallots
4 5-ounce fresh salmon filets,
  skinned
½ teaspoon salt

½ bottle (375 ml.) champagne
2 tablespoons all-purpose flour
1 tablespoon butter,
  at room temperature
¾ cup heavy (whipping) cream

1. Grease bottom of a large skillet with 1 rounded teaspoon butter. Sprinkle shallots over butter. Place salmon filets on top. Sprinkle salmon with salt. Pour champagne over filets. Cover skillet and bring champagne to a boil over high heat. Reduce heat to low and simmer for 3 to 4 minutes. Remove salmon from pan and keep filets warm. Reserve liquid in pan.

2. Combine flour and 2 tablespoons butter to form a paste, or Beurre Manié.

3. Reduce reserved poaching liquid by one-half over high heat. Gradually add Beurre Manie' to sauce, whisking constantly until it is thick and creamy. Use only enough of Beurre Manié to achieve desired consistency. Sauce should not be too loose or too gooey. Add heavy cream, whisking until it is incorporated. Season to taste.

4. Serve sauce over salmon filets. Accompany with boiled parslied potatoes and a complimentary vegetable.

STRAWBERRIES MARTINE

1 cup sour cream
1 tablespoon light brown sugar
2 tablespoons Grand Marnier

Fresh, whole strawberries,
enough for 4 people*

1. Mash brown sugar in a bowl until well separated. Blend in sour cream until smooth. Add Grand Marnier; mix well. Cover and refrigerate until ready to use.

2. Wash and drain strawberries. Arrange strawberries on a serving plate covered with shaved ice. Pour dipping sauce into individual serving bowls. Dip strawberries into sauce.

The Strawberries should be arranged on an attractive platter and placed in the center of the table so that guests may easily help themselves. Place a large white folded cloth napkin on the platter and then cover it with shaved ice. Place strawberries in the ice. Serve each guest the dipping sauce in small individual bowls on dessert plates. They may use the long stem strawberries to dip into the sauce. If you cannot find stemmed strawberries, make sure you supply guests with small cocktail forks.

*Find the largest ripe strawberries you can, preferably with long stems.

Rose et LeFavour

Café Oriental

Dinner for Four

Fresh Duck Foie Gras in a Salad of Local Greens

Papillôte of California King Salmon and Elephant Garlic

Grilled Squab with Spinach and Beurre Blanc

Cheeses

Vanilla Bavarois with Fraises des Bois

WINES:

With the Foie Gras—Robert Mondavi Moscato
D'Oro (375 ml.), 1983

With the Salmon—Freemark Abbey Chardonnay, 1981

With the Squab—Steltzner Vineyards Cabernet Sauvignon, 1981

With the Bavarois—Joseph Phelps Scheurebe
Select Late Harvest, 1982

Bruce LeFavour, Owner and Chef

When Rose et LeFavour opened in 1981, it quickly became the Napa Valley's newest culinary sensation. Bruce LeFavour's own very personal style of cooking–French with a pronounced Oriental influence–won him a loyal following. The intimate restaurant provided a perfect setting for the exquisite six course *prix fixe* dinner he created each evening. Bruce admits to being self-taught as a chef, having learned his craft from reading French technical cookbooks and touring France's three star restaurants on bicycle.

In 1985, his love of travel took him to Thailand, Burma, India, and Sri Lanka. The ideas he brought back contributed to a change in the name, menu, and decor of the restaurant.

He renamed the restaurant Rose et LeFavour Cafe Oriental. The fabric swathed walls were colorfully decorated with beautiful Japanese and Thai robes and large flags of many countries were hung from the high ceiling. LeFavour's own enlarged photographs of Burmese street scenes and food vendors complete the vivid decor.

The biggest change was reflected in the food menu. Although the popular six course *prix fixe* menu was retained, an á la carte menu was added. Dishes like soup of Range Hen in Coconut Milk with Galanga, Poached Farm Eggs with Fennel, Terrine of fresh Duck Foie Gras, and Rhode Island Oysters with Creamed Leeks are unusual and tempting. Issan Souvenir, a participatory dish for two, is a Northern Thailand venison dish served with an array of spicy condiments. Taking comic license, LeFavour recreates the War of 1905, serving Tuna Japanese style with Filet of Beef Russian Style.

A wine list with over 400 selections and an unusually broad depth of vintages compliments the cornucopia of flavors and visual delights created by Chef LeFavour.

1420 Main Street
St. Helena

FRESH DUCK FOIE GRAS IN A SALAD OF LOCAL GREENS

1 teaspoon Dijon mustard
1 shallot, finely minced
1 tablespoon French champagne
vinegar
3 tablespoons Italian virgin olive oil
Mesculin* for 4 salads

Salt and white pepper
Fresh duck foie gras
(4-½ inch thick slices)
1 cup all-purpose flour
1 Daikon radish, peeled**
1 cup all-purpose flour

1. For dressing, mix together mustard, shallot, salt and pepper, and champagne vinegar in a bowl. Slowly whisk in olive oil. Toss mesculin with dressing until greens just glisten. Do not overdress. Reserve remaining dressing.

2. Heat a heavy non-stick skillet over high heat until very hot. Meanwhile, salt and pepper foie gras, then dredge slices in flour. Shake off excess flour, leaving a very thin dusting. Quickly place slices in dry hot pan. As soon as slices brown, about 15 to 30 seconds, turn them over using a spatula. Brown slices on this side, about 15 to 30 seconds. Remove slices from pan.

3. To assemble, place a small pool of remaining dressing on 4 salad plates. Place a slice of foie gras on top of dressing. Arrange dressed greens around foie gras. Using a vegetable peeler, remove 4 long slices of radish; arrange one strip over each salad. Garnish with chives and flowers, if desired.

The Moscato D'Oro, a sweet wine, goes very well with foie gras. The richness of the foie gras seems to modify the sweetness of the wine, leaving the richness and fruit of the wine. If this seems too radical a suggestion, a sparkling wine would be a good choice.

*This salad is a mixture of 6 or 7 different kinds of very young greens, sometimes sold as mesculin, augmented with edible flowers such as chives, day lily, or borage.

**Daikon is a Japanese long white radish and can be purchased in most produce departments.

PAPILLOTE OF CALIFORNIA KING SALMON AND ELEPHANT GARLIC

4 10-inch rounds parchment paper
¼-½ cup butter, melted
2 1-inch thick salmon steaks,
   skin removed and boned
   into 4 pieces
Salt and white pepper to taste

GARLIC BUTTER
2 cloves Elephant garlic*,
   thinly sliced
Pernod liqueur
12 sprigs fresh chervil

1. On a flat surface, liberally coat the parchment paper with melted butter. Place one piece of salmon on lower half of round. Salt and pepper salmon. Smear 1 tablespoon GARLIC BUTTER over each salmon piece. Place 4 slices of garlic around and against sides of salmon but not on top. Sprinkle with a few drops of Pernod. Place 3 sprigs chervil on top of salmon.

2. To make Papillôte, fold the top half of the paper over to meet bottom half. Curved edges will meet exactly. Fold the edges of the paper tightly together to make a package which is airtight and will puff up when heated. Start at the left side of the curved edge and fold edges carefully but firmly inward moving to the right around the curved edge, pressing with thumb while making a series of small folds. Make 3 or 4 folds at the right corner to ensure a good seal. Now, at the right end, proceed back toward the left side, making a series of double folds. Make 3 or 4 folds at the left end to seal. Bake or refrigerate until one hour before cooking.

3. Place oven rack in upper position. Preheat oven to 450 degrees. Bake Papillôte directly on upper rack for 5 minutes. At this point, they should have puffed up. If Papillôte have not puffed, and you can see unmelted butter through the parchment paper on top of the salmon, bake for 1 to 2 minutes longer.

4. To serve, carefully slide each unopened Papillôte on to a heated plate. Serve immediately. The aroma as each guest opens his Papillôte is heavenly.

*If the Papillôte never puffs, you may have a defective seal. The salmon will still cook, but you should remove it from its package before serving.

GARLIC BUTTER

1 clove Elephant garlic*,
 finely chopped
1 shallot, finely chopped
4 sprigs of chervil, finely chopped
 Zest of ½ lemon,
 finely chopped

½ teaspoon Pernod liqueur
4 tablespoons unsalted butter,
 at room temperature
Juice of ½ lemon
Salt and white pepper to taste

1. Combine garlic, shallot, lemon peel, and chervil in a small bowl. Add lemon juice, Pernod, and butter; blending until smooth. Add salt and pepper to taste.

*Elephant garlic is a giant but mild variety of garlic commonly grown in the Napa Valley.

GRILLED SQUAB WITH SPINACH AND BEURRE BLANC

¼ cup finely chopped shallot
½ cup French champagne vinegar
½ cup salted butter,
    cut into chunks
Salt and pepper

4 16-ounce squab,
    breasts removed*
2 large bunches spinach,
    cleaned and stemmed
2 tablespoons unsalted butter

1. Combine shallot and vinegar in a saucepan over low heat until almost all the liquid has evaporated. Remove from heat; cool slightly. Vigorously stir in salted butter and strain before all the butter is melted, pushing down on the shallots to extract all the flavor. (The butter should be heated enough to make it liquid but not so much that it will separate.) Reserve this BEURRE BLANC in a warm, not hot, place.

2. Prepare a hot grill. Salt and pepper squab breasts. Place them, skin side down, on prepared grill. Cook breasts, turning frequently, until medium rare, about 3 to 5 minutes.

3. Meanwhile, melt unsalted butter in a heavy saucepan over high heat. Add spinach and salt and pepper; lightly toss until it begins to cook and wilt. Remove spinach and place a mound of it on 4 heated plates. Place two squab breasts on spinach. Just before serving, pour *BEURRE BLANC* around spinach.

At the Cafe Oriental, they make a quick stock with the browned bodies of the squab and ½ of the legs. They then braise the remaining legs, feet and all, in the stock before grilling them with the breast meat. This is not at all necessary, as there is little meat on the leg. Chef LeFavour just likes the presentation of having a leg, complete with claws, on each plate.

When buying squab, have the butcher remove the breasts from each squab.

VANILLA BAVAROIS WITH FRAISES DES BOIS

1 tablespoon unflavored gelatin
    (1 envelope)
3 tablespoons cold water
1½ cups milk
    vanilla bean, 1 inch piece, split

4 egg yolks (5 if eggs are small)
¾ cup sugar
1½ cups heavy (whipping) cream
1 cup fraises des bois*

1. Butter a 1-quart mold. Sprinkle gelatin over cold water in a cup. Heat gelatin by placing cup in a bowl of hot water; set aside.

2. Scald milk and vanilla bean in a small, heavy saucepan. Set aside for 15 minutes.

3. Meanwhile, beat egg yolks and sugar until light in color. Add egg yolk mixture to hot milk, stirring constantly. Place mixture over low heat, whisking constantly until it thickens and coats the back of a spoon. Immediately strain the mixture into a medium bowl set in a large bowl of ice, stirring constantly. Add gelatin, stirring until mixture cools significantly. Then stir it occasionally as it cools further and begins to stiffen.

4. Beat whipping cream in a chilled bowl with chilled beaters until stiff peaks form. Fold whipped cream, ⅓ at a time, into gelatin mixture. Gently fold in fraises des bois, reserving a few for garnish. Pour mixture into prepared mold; chill for 4 to 5 hours. Unmold before serving.

Prior to dessert, LeFavour offers his guests a selection of 5 or 6 imported and domestic cheeses. Some examples might include raw milk Brie, Oregon Blue, and Vermont Cheddar.

*Says Chef LeFavour,"When I eat dessert, nothing pleases me more than this Bavarois. I came up with the recipe after receiving a overwhelming amount of fraises des bois from our local supplier. It is important to use real fraises des bois, for their distinctive perfume permeates the "pudding" and blends perfectly with the strong vanilla flavor."

CALISTOGA INN

Dinner for Six

Smoked Salmon Mousse with Black Caviar

Red Bell Pepper and Tomato Soup

Braised Sea Bass with Saffron and Mussels

Frozen Blackberry Soufflé

WINES:

With the Salmon Mousse—Markham Sauvignon Blanc, 1984

With the Soup—Raymond Chenin Blanc, 1983

With the Sea Bass—Stonegate Chardonnay, 1983

*With the Soufflé—Long Vineyards Botrytis
Johannisberg Riesling, 1981*

Philip Rogers, Owner and Chef

In early 1979, Phil Rogers bought the Calistoga Inn, and with a bit of elbow grease, transformed the turn of the century building into a charming inn with 17 rooms and a soon-to-be-famous restaurant. The rooms, which have the feel and the price tag of a continental pension or guest house, are nearly always booked and offer an inexpensive and comfortable place for visitors to stay in the Napa Valley.

The restaurant, however, is the focal point of the Calistoga Inn. The menu is weighted to fresh seafood, and changes daily, enabling Phil to take advantage of the finest and freshest fish, seafood, fruits, vegetables, and meats on the seasonal market. The daily menu features at least 10 entrees of fresh fish and a selection of veal, steak, game and pasta. Homemade desserts and a large, comprehensive wine list nicely round out a dinner at Calistoga Inn. Before or after dinner, stop in the adjacent pub-like bar where Phil has built an impressive selection of over 50 beers from around the world.

When asked about his goals for the restaurant, Phil said, "What we strive for is a straightforward, unpretentious approach to food without being trendy. We consistently use only the freshest ingredients in our cooking and impeccably fresh fish. We want people to come back year after year."

Local residents and visitors do repeatedly come back to the Calistoga Inn, enjoying fine food in the simplicity of its Bistro-like dining room or outdoor patio. The restaurant, like the inn, has the comfortable hometown look and feel that is so appropriate in the town of Calistoga.

1250 Lincoln Avenue
Calistoga

SMOKED SALMON MOUSSE WITH BLACK CAVIAR

⅛ pound smoked salmon
  (trimmings are satisfactory)
1 8-ounce package cream cheese
½ teaspoon lemon zest

1 teaspoon lemon juice
1 tablespoon grated red onion
3 tablespoons black Lumpfish caviar,
  rinsed and drained if too salty

1. Purée smoked salmon in a food processor or blender. Add cream cheese, lemon zest, lemon juice, red onion; puree until smooth.

2. Spoon salmon mixture into a pastry bag fitted with a rosette tip. Pipe into decorative mounds on serving plates. Spoon caviar over top.

3. Serve with large croutons or crackers. Garnish with lemon slices, lettuce, and parsley, if desired.

Salmon mousse can be made up to 3 days ahead. Bring mousse up to room temperature before piping it onto serving plates.

RED BELL PEPPER AND TOMATO SOUP

½ pound yellow onions, chopped
2 leeks, chop white part only
⅛ pound unsalted butter
1 pound red bell pepper,
   seeded and deveined*
1 quart chicken stock
½ pound tomatoes, seeded

4 tablespoons olive oil
1 cup heavy (whipping) cream
Dash of cayenne pepper
Dash of white pepper
Dash of salt
Crème Fraîche
  (consult index)

1. Sauté onions and leeks with olive oil in a large skillet over medium heat until limp. Do not brown.

2. Add butter and bell pepper; and "sweat" them on a low flame for 10 minutes.

3. Add chicken stock and bring mixture to a boil.

4. Add tomatoes. Reduce heat to low and simmer for 20 minutes.

5. Pour mixture into a blender or food processor; purée. Strain mixture into a saucepan.

6. Add heavy cream. Heat soup over medium heat. Do not boil. Season with cayenne pepper, white pepper, and salt.

7. Serve warm in soup bowls. Garnish each with a dollop of Crème Fraîche.

*This soup can be made with bell peppers only if desired, just increase peppers by ½ pound.

BRAISED SEA BASS WITH SAFFRON AND MUSSELS

1 cup vermouth
1 teaspoon chopped shallots
1 teaspoon saffron threads
1½ cups fish stock
  or bottled clam juice
6 5-ounce portions of Sea Bass

2-3 tablespoons clarified butter
18 mussels, cleaned and debearded
1½ cups heavy (whipping) cream
  All-purpose flour
  Salt and white pepper

1. Preheat oven to 400 degrees.

2. Combine vermouth, shallots, and saffron in a small saucepan over high heat. Reduce liquid by one-half. Add fish stock. Decrease heat to low and simmer.

3. Lightly dust sea bass with flour, shaking off excess. Sauté bass in clarified butter in a large oven-proof sauté pan for 2 to 3 minutes. Do not brown. (This is just to seal the flesh of the fish.) Pour off any excess butter. Pour saffron mixture over fish.

4. Add mussels to fish mixture. Cover pan with foil. Bake for 5 minutes, or until fish is almost cooked. Do not overbake. Remove from oven and transfer bass and mussels to a heated platter. Remove any unopened mussels and discard.

5. Remove any unopened mussels and discard. Add heavy cream to remaining braising liquid and reduce over high heat until the liquid measures about 1 cup. Season with salt and pepper.

6. To serve, arrange mussels around the bass and pour the sauce over top. Serve with rice. a green vegetable, and a third vegetable of contrasting color.

This is visually a beautiful dish, the black mussels making a striking contrast to the brilliant yellow saffron sauce.

FROZEN BLACKBERRY SOUFFLE

1½ cups heavy (whipping) cream   *Pinch of salt*
3 egg whites   *3 cups blackberries*
½ cup sugar puréed and strained

1. Line a 9 x 5 x 3-inch loaf pan with parchment paper.

2. Beat whipping cream and salt in a chilled bowl with chilled beaters until stiff peaks form. Set aside.

3. Beat egg whites and sugar in a clean bowl with clean beaters until stiff peaks form. Fold egg white mixture into whipped cream, ⅓ at a time.

4. Fold puréed blackerries, 1 cup at a time, into whipped cream mixture.

5. Gently pour mixture into prepared loaf pan. Freeze until hard, about 12 hours. Slice and serve with seasonal berries and fresh mint leaves, if desired.

To unmold, dip the pan briefly into hot water, invert, and remove pan. The soufflé can be unmolded and put back into the freezer for 1-2 hours before serving if desired.

This soufflé can be made with different kinds of berries, but it may be necessary to adjust the sugar depending upon the sweetness of the berries you select.

D.D. KAYS
UPTOWN BAR & GRILL

Dinner for Six

Linguine Roberta

Steamed Blue Maine Mussels

Maple Leaf Duck with Blueberry Sauce

Arugula Salad with Raspberry Vinaigrette

Bread Pudding with Bourbon Sauce

WINES:

With the Linguine—Shramsberg Blanc de Blancs

With the Mussels—ZD Chardonnay, 1983

With the Duck—Cuvaison Zinfandel, 1980

With the Bread Pudding—Cappuccino

Roberta Keller, Dave Cummings, Ken Cummings, and Dave Fyfe
Owners

Peter Di Pasqua, Executive Chef

For years, the town of Napa has needed a restaurant like it, a place with fresh, innovative food in a citified atmosphere conducive to gathering and socializing. Finally in 1984, four enterprising Napans got together and opened D.D. Kay's Uptown Bar and Grill.

They renovated an old, authentic, tile-fronted building in downtown Napa that easily lent itself to an Art Deco theme. Existing rounded soffits were enhanced by recessed lighting that gently washes soft pink walls. Eye-catching touches of drama were added with polished, blue mirrors and blue neon lights shining through old-fashioned glass blocks. The feel is city slick, "uptown", and casually elegant.

Napa has embraced D.D. Kay's wholeheartedly. The restaurant is generally full for lunch, for it sits across the street from the courthouse. It also fills the bill for Napa-based wineries, for the restaurant is peppered with vintners. At night, the place is hopping—full of dinner patrons, as well as those who fill the adjacent bar where some of the best live music in the area is performed five nights a week.

Fortunately, the owners gave ultimate importance to the chef they selected. Young, enthusiastic chef Peter Di Pasqua turns out interesting, well-executed variations on classic themes. The menu offers a variety of fresh fish and meats, and homemade pastas, all garnished whimsically with exotic edible flowers or unusual herbs. "I'm given lots of creative freedom by the owners," says Peter. Each day, in addition to the menu, Peter exercises that creative license, offering four or five specials which are traditionally based, yet with an unusual twist or two in sauce or presentation.

"We want to please", says owner and Maitre D', Dave Cummings. Considering the obvious popularity of D.D. Kay's, I'd say they're succeeding.

811 Coombs Street
Napa

LINGUINE ROBERTA

1 pound fresh linguine
   Dash of oil
1 cup carrots, peeled,
   then halved lengthwise
   and sliced
½ cup broccoli,
   cut into flowerettes
½ cup cauliflower
   cut into flowerettes
1 tablespoon olive oil
1 tablespoon clarified butter
2 large mushroom caps, quartered
1 cup julienned Bermuda onion
1 small green pepper, julienned

1 small red pepper, julienned
1 small zucchini, sliced (or
   use summer or yellow squash)
1 tomato, poached, seeded,
   and quartered
1 tablespoon minced garlic
1 tablespoon minced shallots
2 tablespoons dry sherry
2 tablespoons dry white wine
1 tablespoon unsalted butter
3-4 tablespoons vegetable stock*
1 tablespoon fresh herbs**
Pinch of salt and pepper
Freshly grated Parmesan cheese

1. Blanch the carrots, broccoli, and cauliflower. Drain well. This may be done earlier in the day.

2. In one gallon of boiling salted water with a dash of oil added, cook linguine until *al-dente*. Drain well.

3. Add olive oil and clarified butter to a 14-inch skillet over high heat. Add mushrooms, onions, green pepper, red pepper, and zucchini to hot oil. Sauté one minute. Add broccoli, cauliflower, carrots, tomato, garlic, and shallots. Add a pinch of salt, pepper and herbs. Toss to mix. Add sherry, white wine, butter, and stock. Sauté one minute. Fold in linguine. Cook until pasta is hot.

4. Serve on warm salad-sized plates.

5. Pass the Parmesan cheese at the table.

Any fresh garden vegetables will do for this dish, but try to use a colorful combination.

*At D.D. Kay's, we blanch most of our vegetables, cooling them immediately after in an ice bath to prevent further cooking. We reserve the poaching liquid, or vegetable stock, and use it instead of butter to glaze the pans in which we sauté our vegetables. This adds a refreshing flavor.

**Fresh herbs including marjoram, thyme, oregano, savory, or sage

STEAMED BLUE MAINE MUSSELS

2 tablespoons minced garlic
2 tablespoons minced shallots
3 cups dry white wine
1 cup heavy (whipping) cream
¼ cup dry vermouth
4-5 medium Eastern mussels per person, cleaned and bearded

½ cup chopped sorrel
1 teaspoon salt
2 teaspoons black pepper
½ cup lemon juice
½ cup chopped chervil*
Pinch of finely chopped assorted herbs

1. Combine garlic, shallots, dry white wine, heavy cream, Vermouth, sorrel, chervil, salt, black pepper, lemon juice, and pinch of assorted herbs. Bring to a boil.

2. Add mussels. Cover and cook for 3 to 5 minutes over high heat. Check the mussels during the cooking time, removing the ones that have opened to a warm, stainless steel bowl.

3. Meanwhile, warm 6 serving bowls.

4. Arrange 4 to 5 mussels in each bowl. Discard any mussels that do not open.

5. Reduce remaining liquid by one-quarter. Spoon reduced broth over mussels.

Serve with lots of crusty French bread to soak up the delicious broth.

*Fresh chervil imparts an anise flavor to the sauce. If you do not have fresh chervil, add a dash of Pernod or Ricard liqueur to the poaching liquid.

MAPLE LEAF DUCK WITH BLUEBERRY SAUCE
BLUEBERRY SAUCE

1 8-ounce jar currant jelly
1 cup duck or chicken broth
3 pints fresh blueberries
2 tablespoons Blackberry brandy

2 cups Zinfandel wine
3 tablespoons arrowroot
   or cornstarch
¼ cup red or white wine

1. Heat currant jelly in a 2 quart saucepan. Add duck or chicken broth, reserving ¼ cup, and 2 pints blueberries. Bring to a boil, then reduce heat and simmer for 5 minutes.

2. Pour mixture into a blender. Purée until smooth.

3. Return mixture to saucepan and simmer 2 minutes.

4. Add brandy and 1½ cups Zinfandel wine. Add one-half of remaining pint of blueberries, reserving rest for garnish.

5. Dilute arrowroot in ¼ cup wine and add to sauce. Cook for 2 minutes. (If the sauce becomes too thick, thin with more stock.)

6. Add sugar, one teaspoon at a time, to mellow flavor if sauce tastes too tart. Set aside.

DUCK

¼ cup olive oil
3-4 pound Maple Leaf
   or Long Island ducks*

Salt and pepper to taste

1. Preheat oven to 500 degrees.

2. Heat olive oil until smoking in a 14-inch aluminum skillet. Salt and pepper both sides of duck and place it skin side down into skillet. Sear one side.

3. Bake duck seared side up in pan for 5 minutes. Remove from oven and drain off all the fat.

4. Return duck to oven and bake for 4 minutes.

5. Remove from oven and add remaining ½ cup Zinfandel, salt and pepper, and 1 cup BLUEBERRY SAUCE to skillet.

6. Bake for 2 minutes, or until duck feels plump and firm. Duck will be medium-rare to medium.

7. Serve with rice and vegetables.

To serve, place rice to one side of plate, and vegetable to other side. Place one leg on top of rice at a right angle. Slice breasts into 4 or 5 strips, fanning them out directly below leg. Place 1 to 2 ounces of BLUEBERRY SAUCE over duck, but do not smother.

*Have your butcher remove the breasts and legs from each duck, removing also the thigh bone but leaving the drumstick in. Leave enough fat on the breasts to cover the perimeter.

ARUGULA SALAD WITH RASPBERRY VINAIGRETTE

¼ cup raspberry vinegar
¾ cup olive oil or walnut oil
½ tablespoon pesto sauce (optional)
1 tablespoon fresh herbs*
1 teaspoon minced garlic
1 teaspoon minced shallot
¼ teaspoon salt

¼ cup CREME FRAICHE, consult index
1 tablespoon Dijon mustard
Freshly ground white pepper
6 bunches arugula
6 ounces Bucheron (goat cheese)
1 dozen round croutons**

1. Combine raspberry vinegar, olive oil, pesto sauce, herbs, garlic, shallots, salt, mustard, and white pepper to taste.

2. Blend in crème fraîche. (The dressing should be creamy, but not thick.) Set aside.

3. Gently wash arugula in ice water. If roots are small and tender leave them on. If not, remove them. Drain in a large colander.

4. Preheat oven to 350 degrees. Bake Bucheron until soft, about 5 minutes.

5. Spread softened cheese over croutons.

6. To serve, toss arugula with VINAIGRETTE in a salad bowl. Do not overdress. Arrange greens on cool salad plates. Place 2 croutons on each plate and serve.

This makes a wonderful luncheon salad with the addition of one smoked poussin, cut into pieces and arranged on top of the dressed arugula.

*Select fresh herbs of your choice.

**To make croutons, cut a baguette into thin slices and toast under broiler.

BREAD PUDDING WITH BOURBON SAUCE

1 loaf stale French bread
5 cups milk
1 cup heavy (whipping) cream
7 eggs, lightly beaten
1 cup coarsely chopped walnuts
1 cup raisins or currants

1 cup sugar
2 teaspoons nutmeg
1 tablespoon cinnamon
BOURBON SAUCE
Mint leaves, for garnish
Whipped cream, for garnish

1. Grease a 9x13x2-inch baking pan. Preheat oven to 325 degrees.

2. Cut French bread into cubes. Place bread cubes in a large mixing bowl. Combine milk and heavy cream in a small bowl; pour over bread cubes.

3. Add lightly beaten eggs to bread mixture; blend well. Stir in walnuts and raisins.

4. Combine sugar, nutmeg, and cinnamon in a small bowl.

5. Arrange one-half of bread mixture on bottom of prepared pan. Sprinkle one-half of sugar mixture over bread cubes. Turn remaining bread mixture into pan. Top with remaining sugar mixture.

6. Place baking pan in a ¼-inch water bath. Bake, covered with aluminum foil, for 40 minutes. Remove foil and bake an additional 15 minutes, or until browned and firmly set.

7. To serve, preheat oven to 500 degrees. Place a spoonful of BOURBON SAUCE on the bottom of 6 ovenproof dessert plates. Place a piece of pudding on top. Spoon additional sauce over pudding. Bake for 5 minutes, or until sauce begins to bubble. Serve immediately. Garnish with mint leaf and whipped cream, if desired.

The bread pudding can be made ahead of time and reheated. If you plan to serve the pudding immediately, raise oven temperature to 500 degrees while you prepare the BOURBON SAUCE.

D.D. KAY'S UPTOWN BAR AND GRILL

BOURBON SAUCE

1 cup butter
2 cups confectioners' sugar

1 egg
¼ cup Bourbon

1. Melt butter in a saucepan over low heat. Remove from heat.

2. Gradually sift confectioners' sugar into melted butter, stirring constantly. Add egg. Mix in Bourbon.

THE DINER

Dinner for Six

Fresh Tomato and Corn Salad with Basil and Garlic

Sopa de Chili Verde

Grilled Tuna with Sunshine Salsa

Grilled Vegetables with Herb Butter

Parslied Rice

The Diner's Famous Flan

WINES:

With the Soup—Chappellet Chenin Blanc, 1983

With the Tuna—Louis Martini Zinfandel, 1982

Cassandra Mitchell, Nickie Hamilton, and Kay Frame
Owners

Cassandra Mitchell, Chef

On a rusty, weathered pole outside a painted, block building hangs a sign that reads 'DINER-HOME COOKING'. Here, where for some thirty-odd years folks stopped for a bite while waiting for the Greyhound bus, now sits one of the Napa Valley's most popular gathering spots for hearty breakfasts and wholesome lunches and dinners.

The Diner, built in 1946, began its most recent incarnation in 1975, when San Francisco native Cassandra Mitchell took over. A major facelift was the first order of business, and then the menu was overhauled, and now includes not only popular American standards such as juicy cheeseburgers and creamy buttermilk milkshakes, but also an eclectic collection of recipes such as German Potato Pancakes and Huevos Rancheros. From a seat at the counter you can see into the kitchen where a busy team of cooks prepare an array of foods from home-fried potatoes and fresh squeezed orange juice, to Carne Asada and Chicken and Cream Enchiladas. Many of these people have worked here together for years, helping create the warm family atmosphere that pervades.

"This is a California Diner, complete with palm trees and our own organic garden," says owner/chef Mitchell. "The food is fresh and pure, and our community comes here for all occasions, from the morning espresso and newspaper to a special Saturday night date." Cassandra gets her creative inspiration not only from travels in Mexico, but also from the energetic and inventive Bay Area restaurant scene. She herself is a painter and musician in addition to being a chef, and uses her education at the San Francisco Art Institute to help determine the decor, landscape, and menu of The Diner.

"The Diner's menu reflects my current favorite recipes. The ingredients are as good and as fresh as we can get, which, in California, means the best. We are not trendy, however. The Diner is more like your best fantasy of an American classic." Every evening The Diner is transformed into El Diner, serving up some of the best Mexican food around. The following recipes have a subtle Mexican theme, and make for a marvelous barbecue.

6476 Washington Street
Yountville

FRESH TOMATO AND CORN SALAD WITH BASIL AND GARLIC

5-6 medium, vine-ripened tomatoes,
    preferably warm from the garden
    1 head of lettuce

2 ears of corn,
(or ¾ cup kernels)
VINAIGRETTE

1. Core and cut tomatoes into wedges. Cut corn kernels from the cob, reserving 2 to 3 tablespoons for garnish.

2. Toss tomatoes with VINAIGRETTE in a bowl. Add corn and toss.

3. Arrange lettuce leaves on 6 salad plates. Arrange tomatoes and corn on top.

4. Sprinkle reserved kernels over salad.

VINAIGRETTE

¼ cup virgin olive oil
1 tablespoon seasoned rice vinegar*
1 tablespoon raspberry vinegar
½ teaspoon sea salt

¼ teaspoon freshly ground pepper
½ teaspoon pressed garlic,
  about 1 large clove
2 teaspoons minced fresh basil
  (substitute 1 teaspoon dried)

1. Combine olive oil, rice vinegar, raspberry vinegar, sea salt, pepper, garlic, and basil in a bowl just before serving.

   * *Rice wine vinegar is available in specialty stores. It is most commonly used to prepare sushi rice.*

SOPA DE CHILE VERDE

2 pounds Pasilla chilis
(or 1 27-ounce can green chilis, whole or strips)
1½ quarts chicken stock, homemade or canned
1 cup heavy whipping cream or CREME FRAICHE
Salt and pepper to taste
Sour cream, for garnish
Monterey Jack cheese, for garnish

1. Roast chilis on a cookie sheet under the broiler, turning until evenly blistered and browned. Cover with a towel for 5 minutes and allow to steam until soft. Peel carefully, removing seeds and stem.

2. Cook chilis and chicken stock in a soup pot over medium heat for 20 minutes.

3. Remove chilis from stock and purée in a blender until smooth. Strain chilis into stock.

4. Add cream and salt and pepper to chili mixture. Reheat over medium heat. Serve.

5. Garnish soup with a dollop of sour cream, CREME FRAICHE, or grated Monterey Jack cheese.

Yield: 2 quarts.

CREME FRAICHE

1 teaspoon buttermilk   *1 cup heavy (whipping) cream*

1. Combine buttermilk and heavy cream in a jar. Let mixture stand loosely covered at room temperature until thickened, about 18 to 24 hours.

Crème Fraîche keeps in refrigerator for about 10 days.

GRILLED TUNA WITH SUNSHINE SALSA

1 cup finely minced white onion
⅓ cup seasoned rice wine vinegar
½ cup fresh orange juice
   Juice of 1 lemon
   Zests of 2 lemons,
   with no white pith, finely minced

1 tablespoon minced fresh ginger
2 tablespoons minced orange zest
2 oranges, completely peeled
   and coarsely chopped
6 6 to 8-ounce tuna steaks or fillets
   Olive oil

1. Combine onion and vinegar in a bowl. Blend in orange juice, lemon juice, lemon zest, ginger, orange zest, and oranges. Set aside.

2. Prepare a hot gas or charcoal grill. (If no grill is available, the fish can be cooked under the broiler.)

3. Rub tuna steaks with olive oil. Place fish on hot grill and cook until tuna is just opaque in the center, turning once.

4. Serve immediately with prepared salsa.

Yield: 2 cups Sunshine Salsa.

Sunshine Salsa can be made a day in advance.

PARSLIED RICE

2½ cups long grain brown rice,
    washed and drained well
1 tablespoon oil
3½ cups water
2 teaspoons concentrated chicken
    base or 3 chicken or vegetable
    bouillon cubes, optional

1 tablespoon butter
2 tablespoons minced parsley

1. Sauté rice with oil in a saucepan with a tight fitting lid, turning often until golden brown.

2. Combine water and chicken base. Add mixture to hot rice. Cover saucepan and bring mixture to a boil. Reduce heat to low and cook for 45 minutes. Turn off heat and allow rice to sit for 15 to 20 minutes.

3. Toss butter and parsley into rice mixture. Serve immediately.

GRILLED VEGETABLES WITH HERB BUTTER

6 small eggplants,
   4 to 5 inches long
1 large zucchini,
   12 to 16 inches long
   or 2 medium sized
¼ cup olive oil
   HERB BUTTER

2 tablespoons seasoned
   rice wine vinegar
½ teaspoon Dijon mustard
½ teaspoon minced garlic
   Salt and pepper to taste
6 fresh pimentos or red bell
   peppers

1. Cut eggplants lengthwise into ¼-inch slices, leaving each one connected at stem, so that slices fan apart. Cut large zucchini across or diagonally into ½-inch slices, about 4 inches long.

2. Combine olive oil, rice vinegar, mustard, garlic, and salt and pepper in a bowl.

3. Fan out eggplants and rub with vinaigrette. Rub zucchini with vinaigrette. Set aside.

4. Prepare a hot gas or charcoal grill. (If no grill is available, vegetables can also be cooked under the broiler.)

5. Roast pimentos over hot grill, until evenly blackened. Remove from heat and place in a bowl. Cover bowl and cool for 15 to 30 minutes. When pimentos are cool enough to handle, remove from bowl and peel, leaving seeds and stems intact. (Running water helps in the peeling process, but may take away some of the flavor.)

6. Cook eggplants and zucchini on hot grill, turning often until they are browned, about 10 minutes. Reheat pimentos until warm but not browned.

7. Remove vegetables to warm serving plate and brush with HERB BUTTER.

THE DINER

HERB BUTTER

½ cup butter, at room temperature   1 medium clove garlic, pressed
1 teaspoon minced chives   1 teaspoon minced parsley

1. Blend butter, chives. garlic, and parsley in a small bowl until smooth.

HERB BUTTER is wonderful on grilled French bread as well. Cut a loaf into 1-inch slices, brush with the herb butter, and place on grill. Toast until lightly browned.

THE DINER'S FAMOUS FLAN

1 cup sugar	*½ cinnamon stick*
½ cup water	*3 eggs*
1 cup milk	*2 egg yolks*
1 cup half and half	*⅓ cup sugar*
1 vanilla bean	*1 tablespoon brandy*

1. Melt sugar in a dry skillet over low heat, stirring often. Add water to melted sugar, blend well. Simmer syrup for 10 minutes. Remove from heat; cool slightly.

2. Pour enough syrup to coat the bottom of 6 ramekins, about 1 ounce. Set aside to cool.

3. Preheat oven to 325 degrees. Combine half and half, vanilla bean, and cinnamon stick in a saucepan. Scald mixture over medium heat. Remove from heat and cool for 10 minutes; strain.

4. Combine eggs, egg yolks, sugar, and brandy in a small bowl. Slowly beat warmed milk mixture into egg mixture until well blended.

5. Carefully pour ½ cup custard mixture over syrup in each ramekin. Do not mix syrup and custard. Place ramekins in a water bath and bake for 50 minutes, or until set. Serve warm or cool.

6. To serve, run a table knife around inside of each ramekin. Invert onto serving plates. The syrup will remain liquid and will run down the sides of the custard.

This flan can be made up to 3 days in advance and kept covered in the refrigerator.

Domaine Chandon

Dinner for Six

La Crème de Tomates en Croûte

Les Saint Jacques Marinées aux Deux Citrons et Coriandre

Le Magret de Canard au Cabernet Avec Les Chanterelles

La Crème Glacée aux Framboises Dans Son Sac en Chocolat

WINES

With the Soupe—Chandon Blanc de Noirs

With the St. Jacques—Chandon Reserve

With the Canard—Mount Veeder Cabernet Sauvignon, 1981

With the Crème Glacée—Chandon Brut

Philippe Jeanty, Chef de Cuisine

T aking an afternoon or evening to visit Domaine Chandon is always special for Napa Valley residents, and a "must do" for visitors. Domaine Chandon produces outstanding sparkling wines through the traditional "méthode champenoise" under the expert guidance of its French parent company, Moët-Hennessey.

Take a stroll around the grounds of this beautiful property, along its lily-studded duck ponds, through the Champagne mini-museum displaying 19th century wine presses and other antique winery tools, or relax on the terrace of the Salon over a glass (or two!) of delicious sparkling wine. Here you will be surrounded by the countryside and vineyard views.

Domaine Chandon is first and foremost a winery, yet it also houses a first rate French restaurant serving lunch and dinner from a menu that changes with the bounty of the four seasons. The elegant and spacious dining room is decorated in a rich green that, along with an abundance of glass, seems to bring the out-of-doors inside.

The restaurant finds its direction and inspiration from Chef de Cuisine, Philippe Jeanty. Jeanty, who hails from Epernay and has been with the restaurant since it opened in 1977, trained in France under Moët et Chandon's chef, Joseph Thuet. Thuet, considered to be the best chef in Champagne, taught Jeanty well, for he creates beautifully subtle Champagne sauces and dishes that showcase the winery's own sparkling wines. Jeanty carefully designs his menus with a light adept hand. Says Jeanty, "My cooking is classically French adapted to highlight the abundant variety of California ingredients."

California Drive
Yountville, California

LA CREME DE TOMATES EN CROUTE
Cream of Tomato Soup in Puff Pastry

*1 pound yellow onions,
  peeled and chopped*
4 tablespoons unsalted butter
*3 pounds fresh tomatoes
  quartered**
6 cloves garlic, peeled
*1 bay leaf
  Pinch of thyme, preferably fresh
  Salt and white pepper to taste*
3 cups heavy (whipping) cream

*2 pounds puff pastry
  store-bought or homemade*
1 egg beaten with 1 tablespoon water
*1 carrot, thinly julienned,
  for garnish*
*1 leek, thinly julienned,
  for garnish*
*½ small onion,
  cut into very thin rings,
  for garnish*

1. Cook onions with butter in a 2 to 3 quart saucepan over medium heat until soft. Add tomatoes, garlic, bay leaf, thyme, and salt and pepper and continue to cook uncovered over low heat for 3½ hours. Purée mixture in a blender or food processor; strain. Add heavy cream and salt and pepper. Set aside.

2. Roll puff pastry out to ⅛-inch thickness. Brush surface with egg wash. Using a sharp knife, cut circles of pastry about 2 inches larger in diameter than the ovenproof soup crocks in which the soup will be served.

3. Pour cooled soup into crocks. Divide julienned carrots, onions, and leeks among the crocks. Lay a circle of puff pastry, egg-wash side down, on top of crock and stretch it tight (as for a drum head) and down the sides. Cover and refrigerate crocks for 1 hour.

4. Preheat oven to 450 degrees. Brush egg-wash over pastry top. Bake for 15 minutes, or until light brown. Do not open oven during baking, or the pastry will fall. Serve immediately.

Individual soup crocks can be prepared 1 to 2 days in advance.

*If tomatoes are not very ripe, add 1 tablespoon tomato paste to the soup.

LES SAINT JACQUES MARINEES AUX DEUX CITRONS ET CORIANDRE
(Marinated Scallops in Lemon, Lime, Orange and Cilantro)

1 pound scallops,*
   trimmed and cleaned
   Cut in half if large
¼ cup lemon juice
¼ cup lime juice
¼ cup orange juice
¼ bundle fresh cilantro
   (Chinese Parsley), chopped
1 cucumber, unpeeled and
   sliced into paper thin rounds
1 red onion, very thinly sliced
   Fresh chives, chopped

2 avocados, peeled and
   sliced into wedges
¼ cup red wine vinegar
¼ cup plus 2 tablespoons champagne
1 ounce Sevruga caviar, for garnish
¼ cup sour cream
2 ounces golden caviar
½ cup olive oil
   Orange zest, julienned
   Lemon zest, julienned
   Lime zest, julienned

1. Marinate scallops in lemon juice, lime juice, orange juice, and cilantro in a bowl; cover and refrigerate for 3 to 4 hours.

2. Meanwhile, marinate onion slices in vinegar in a bowl for 3 hours; drain. Arrange onions in a ring on serving plates. Line individual custard cups with slightly overlapping very thin slices of cucumbers.

3. Drain scallops. Firmly press scallops into custard cups; invert and unmold onto the center of serving plates. Place 3 slices of avocado around the scallop mold. Sprinkle chives around the outside of onion rings. Place a pinch of lemon zest, lime zest, and orange zest on top of scallops; set aside.

4. Crush golden caviar in a bowl with a wire whisk. Slowly add oil, whisking constantly. Add sour cream and champagne. Place a small dollop of dressing at each end of the avocado slices. Garnish with Sevruga caviar.

*You may substitute fresh salmon filet for the scallops, cutting salmon into pieces the size of scallops. Or use a combination of scallops and salmon.

DOMAINE CHANDON

LE MAGRET DE CANARD AU CABERNET AVEC LES CHANTERELLES
Duck Breast with Cabernet and Chanterelles

6 duck breasts,
  removed from 3 ducks
  (used in DEMI-GLACE)
2 pounds fresh chanterelles,
  sliced
Water

3 cloves garlic, chopped
½ cup butter
3 shallots, chopped
2 cups DEMI-GLACE*
  Salt and pepper to taste

1. Preheat oven to 500 degrees. Meanwhile, heat an ovenproof sauté pan over medium-high heat. Salt and pepper duck breasts. Lay breasts in hot sauté pan, skin side down. No oil or fat is needed. Cook until breasts begin to take color; transfer pan into oven. Bake for 8 minutes, or until medium rare. Remove from oven. Set aside; keep breasts warm.

2. Sauté chanterelles, shallots, and garlic with 6 tablespoons butter in a sauté pan over medium heat. Add a little water and cook for 15 minutes. Add remaining 2 tablespoons butter and salt and pepper. Set aside.

3. To serve, slice duck breasts, and fan each breast out on plate. Sauce duck with DEMI-GLACE, covering it only partially. Ladle chanterelles and juices on top of duck.

Accompaniments on the plate might include carrot purée, garlic purée, and julienned zucchini sautéed in butter.

The most important part of this dish is the stock, which forms the basis of the sauce. It is a time-consuming and costly process, but there are no short cuts that yield similar results. It is worth every effort.

STOCK AND DEMI-GLACE

2 pounds veal bones, with
  cartilage attached
Bones from 3 ducks
1 tablespoons unsalted butter
  or oil
2 large yellow onions,
  cut into large cubes
3 large carrots,
  cut into large cubes

1 head of garlic
10 black peppercorns
3 bay leaves
1 sprig of thyme
  (fresh if available)
4 ripe tomatoes, chopped roughly
2 tablespoons tomato paste
2 fifths good quality
  Cabernet Sauvignon

1. Preheat oven to 425 degrees. Remove duck breasts, trimming excess fat around edges. Set aside. Cut duck carcasses and legs into 7 or 8 pieces each. In a roasting pan, combine veal and duck bones and roast until golden brown.

2. Meanwhile, warm a 3 gallon stock pot over low heat. Add butter or oil. Add onions, carrots, garlic, peppercorns, bay leaves, thyme, and tomatoes to melted butter; "sweat" for 10 minutes.

3. Add tomato paste and "sweat" for an additional 5 minutes.

4. Add roasted bones, being sure to leave fat behind in roasting pan. Mix bones and vegetables for 5 minutes.

5. Add wine. Increase heat to medium and reduce wine for 15 minutes.

6. Add enough water to cover bones. Bring stock to a slow simmer and cook uncovered for 8 hours. Continue to add water as needed to keep bones covered.

7. Do not stir! Skim off fat and scum as it rises to surface during cooking process. After 8 hours, stock should be dark and clear. (If necessary, stock can be turned off overnight and returned to simmer the next day.)

8. Strain mixture without pressing. The liquid (approximately 10 cups) is the stock. Discard the rest. Place stock in stock pot over low heat and reduce to 2 cups , or until thick and rich in flavor, about 3 to 4 hours. This is the DEMI-GLACE.

DEMI-GLACE is meat stock that has been cooked down very slowly, uncovered, until it has solidified and has formed a glutinous substance that will coat a spoon. It may be purchased in some gourmet food shops.

LA CREME GLACEE AUX FRAMBOISES DANS SON SAC EN CHOCOLAT
Raspberry Milkshake in a Chocolate Bag

6 paper coffee bags
  with wax lining
2 pounds Belgian dark chocolate
  (Bittersweet Couverture), chopped
3 baskets fresh raspberries,
  or frozen if fresh unavailable
  Granulated sugar to taste
½ gallon vanilla ice cream,
  preferably homemade

1 cup milk
3 teaspoons lemon juice
¼ cup plus 2 tablespoons
  raspberry liqueur
6 Peruvian lilies, or other fresh
  non-poisonous flowers
6 fern tips
  Raspberries
18 small Palmiers cookies
6 straws*

1. Cut paper bags about 3½-inches high with pinking shears. Open bags; set aside.

2. Melt chocolate in a double boiler over simmering water. Stir until barely melted. Remove top of double boiler and stir constantly until chocolate cools, about 10 minutes. Then again place top of double boiler over simmering water for about 5 seconds. Fill paper bags half-full with melted chocolate. Quickly turn bags over, making sure that the chocolate thinly coats the entire inside of the bag. Fill in cracks with chocolate using a ¼-inch paintbrush or coat entire surface twice. Chill for 5 minutes, or until chocolate is set. Store in refrigerator or freezer until ready to use.

3. Cook raspberries in a small saucepan over medium heat for 15 minutes. Add sugar, if necessary, depending on how sweet raspberries are. Combine raspberries, ice cream, milk, lemon juice, and raspberry liqueur until smooth in a blender. (This may have to be done in batches.)

4. Gently peel paper off chocolate bags. Place chocolate bag on a serving plate. Fill bag three-quarter full with raspberry milkshake. Inside the bag, place a straw on one side and a lily on the other side. Place a fern tip with a few raspberries on the plate, to the right of the bag. Arrange 3 cookies on the left side.

Chocolate bags can be frozen up to 1 week.

*Silver straws with a spoon at the end are preferrable. If you find them please let Philippe Jeanty know.

THE FRENCH LAUNDRY MENU

Dinner for Six

Warm Salad of Sweetbreads and Mushrooms

Sorrel Soup

Aunt Polly's Braised Lamb Shanks

Simple Green Salad with Cheeses

Rhubarb Shortcake

WINES:

With the Sweetbreads—S. Anderson Estate
Bottled Chardonnay, 1983

With the Lamb Shanks—Stags' Leap Vintners Petite Syrah, 1980

With the Shortcake—Robert Pecota Muscato di Andrea, 1984

Don and Sally Schmitt, Owners

Sally Schmitt, Chef

Having dinner with Don and Sally Schmitt at the French Laundry is like being invited into their home for a dinner party. In a rustic, old, fieldstone building that formerly housed an authentic French Laundry, is now one of the Napa Valley's best restaurants and also one of it's best kept secrets.

Each evening there is one seating for dinner, with guests arriving between 7:00 and 8:30. Don, the affable host, greets guests and explains that the restaurant is theirs for the entire evening. He encourages them to walk around the restaurant, linger on the decks that wrap around the upper level of the house, stroll outside in their charming flower garden, or say hello to Sally in the kitchen. Don't linger too long though, if you want your dinner!

Sally, who is the motherly, twinkly-eyed chef, confesses, "I hate a kitchen with a high tech look." Understandable, for her kitchen is homey and immaculate, with polished hardwood floors, fresh herbs in earthenware pots, bowls of perfectly ripened fruit, and a large island around which the staff gathers daily for prep work. On any given afternoon, you will find Sally and her young staff, hands busy, all involved in lively conversation that includes a wide variety of topics. The young people who work at The French Laundry are like family. In fact, three of the Schmitt's five children work in the restaurant. They all perform a variety of jobs, from preparation and cleanup to arranging flowers and serving guests. Don and Sally create a loving environment and needless to say, it shows up at the table.

Much like a dinner party, one five-course menu is prepared each evening, although guests have a choice of appetizer and dessert. The cooking at the French Laundry might be described as refined American cooking. Sally draws from her family (her Mother and relatives) as the source of some of her recipes, modernizing them to take advantage of new ideas. Her style is fresh and straightforward, and all dishes are homemade in her special 'hands on' way.

The following menu is typical of an evening repast at the French Laundry. Sally recommends this menu for an evening in late winter.

6640 Washington Street
Yountville

WARM SALAD OF SWEETBREADS AND MUSHROOMS

2 pairs sweetbreads
1 lemon, sliced
⅓ cup butter
  Zest of 1 lemon
  Juice of 1 lemon
¼ cup chopped Italian parsley
2 tbsp. chopped fresh thyme
  Salt and freshly ground pepper

4 strips thickly sliced bacon, cut
  into small pieces and fried crisp
2 bunches green onions
6 very large or 12 large
  mushroom caps
1 bunch watercress
  Pink peppercorns
1 lemon, sliced

1. Soak sweetbreads in cold water for 1 hour.

2. Add sweetbreads and 1 sliced lemon to a pan of simmering water. Simmer for 15 minutes. Immediately transfer sweetbreads to a pan of ice water.

3. When cool enough to handle, remove all outer tissue and connecting tubes and separate into bite-sized pieces. Refrigerate until ready to use.

4. Melt butter in a sauté pan over medium heat until foaming. Add sweetbreads and quickly brown them over a medium-high heat.

5. Transfer sweetbreads to a large bowl. Save pan for later use.

6. Add lemon zest, lemon juice, parsley, thyme, bacon, and a generous amount of salt and pepper to sweetbreads; mix well. Season to taste. Set aside.

7. Sauté green onions in a pan used for sweetbread mixture until wilted. Add to sweetbread mixture. Season generously with salt and pepper. Set aside.

8. Before serving, sauté mushroom caps quickly in butter until just heated through.

9. To serve, arrange sprigs of watercress on each plate. Add mushroom caps. Fill with sweetbread mixture. Sprinkle with a few pink peppercorns. This dish is best served warm, not hot.

The sweetbread mixture can be prepared ahead and allowed to rest at room temperature. This improves the flavor.

If the sweetbread mixture has cooled too much, gently warm it in a slow oven before assembly. Except for mushroom caps, this dish can be made a day ahead.

SORREL SOUP

3 medium russet potatoes,
  peeled and sliced
4 cups chicken stock or water
  (or ½ stock, ½ water)
Salt and freshly ground pepper

2 cups light cream
½ cup butter, melted
2 cups packed sorrel leaves,
  washed and stripped off rib

1. Combine potatoes, stock, and salt and pepper in a large soup pot. Cover and bring to a boil. Reduce heat to low and cook gently until potatoes are well done. Remove from heat. Allow potatoes to cool.

2. When potatoes are cool enough to handle, puree potatoes and all liquid in a blender.

3. Combine pureed potatoes and cream. Thin to desired consistency with additional cream.

4. Combine melted butter and sorrel leaves in a blender until all leaves are pureed. (This process will lock the color in and the sorrel will not turn "Army green".) Add to soup.

5. Season with salt and pepper to taste. Heat gently before serving.

*To strip sorrel leaves off their rib, hold stem in one hand and with other hand gently pull down on the leaf

AUNT POLLY'S BRAISED LAMB SHANKS

6 medium lamb shanks
¼ cup lemon juice
1½ cups onions
1½ cup carrot
1½ cup celery
4 cloves garlic, sliced
4 tablespoons butter Parsley, chopped

Salt and freshly ground pepper
½ cup olive oil
3 sprigs fresh mint
2 bay leaves
1½ cup beef consommé
1½ cup red wine

1. Rub lamb shanks with lemon juice. Set aside.

2. Cut onions in half lengthwise, then place cut side on table and slice lengthwise to make match stick sized pieces. Cut carrots and celery into 2 to 3-inch lengths and then cut lengthwise into pieces to match onions.

3. Sauté onions and garlic in butter in a sauté pan until limp and transparent. Add carrots and celery and toss until hot and coated with butter. Salt and pepper vegetables to taste. Cover and set aside.

4. Heat olive oil in a heavy skillet until hot. Brown lamb shanks on all sides. Transfer lamb shanks to a large covered casserole. Salt and pepper thoroughly. Cover shanks with vegetables. Place bay leaves and mint sprigs on top.

5. Preheat oven to 350 degrees. Pour oil out of skillet. Add consommé and wine and bring to a boil. Pour over shanks. Cover and bake for 3 to 4 hours.

6. When shanks are very tender, pour the juices off into a large measuring cup. This makes it easier to skim the fat off the top. Season to taste with salt and pepper. Pour juices back into casserole. Set aside. (An hour of rest will improve the lamb's flavor and texture.)

7. Serve one lamb shank on each hot plate. Spoon vegetables over top of each and sprinkle with parsley. Rice or a small pasta such as Semi de Mellone makes a good accompaniment. Spoon juices over all.

SIMPLE GREEN SALAD

1 tablespoon white wine vinegar   ⅔ cup olive oil
2 tablespoons lemon juice   Romaine or other fresh
   Salt and pepper   garden greens

1. Combine vinegar, lemon juice, and olive oil in a small bowl. Season with salt and pepper to taste.

2. Toss dressing and torn salad greens together in a salad bowl.

The French Laundry offers a selection of three cheese with the salad course: a medium aged Asiago, Blue Castello, and St. André. Crisp toast rounds* are also served.

*To make toast rounds, thinly slice a baguette and brush one side with melted butter. Place on a baking sheet in a 300 degree oven for about one hour, or until golden brown and crisp.

RHUBARB SHORTCAKE

BISCUITS

2 cups all-purpose flour	½ cup butter
⅓ cup sugar	1 egg, lightly beaten
1 tablespoon baking powder	½ cup plus 2 tablespoons
½ teaspoon freshly grated nutmeg	light cream

1. Grease a baking sheet. Preheat oven to 400 degrees.

2. Toss together flour, sugar, baking powder, and nutmeg in a bowl. Cut in butter with a pastry blender or two knives used scissor-fashion until mixture resembles fine crumbs.

3. Combine egg and cream; quickly stir into flour mixture with a fork.

4. Drop by forkfuls onto prepared baking sheet. Bake for 15 minutes, or until light brown.

Yield: 12 biscuits

RHUBARB TOPPING

4 cups fresh rhubarb, cut into 1-inch pieces	½ cup Bargetto raspberry wine or orange juice (optional)
1 cup sugar	Heavy (whipping) cream, for garnish

1. Preheat oven to 350 degrees.

2. Combine rhubarb, sugar, and raspberry wine in an ovenproof pan with lid. Bake, covered, for 15 to 30 minutes,* or until rhubarb is tender. Do not stir so that the rhubarb retains its shape.

* Cooking time may vary, depending on the source of the rhubarb.

CARAMEL SAUCE

2 tablespoons butter
½ cup brown sugar

2 tablespoons heavy (whipping)
cream

Combine butter, brown sugar, and heavy cream in a saucepan. Bring to a boil and serve immediately.

TO ASSEMBLE:

1. Warm biscuits in a 350 degree oven until crisp, about 5 to 10 minutes.

2. Split biscuits in half. Place 1 half on dessert plates and spoon warm rhubarb over biscuits. Replace top of biscuit and spoon more rhubarb over top.

3. Pour a spoonful of hot caramel sauce over rhubarb.

4. To garnish, pour heavy cream over sauce, if desired. Serve immediately.

Mama Nina's

Dinner for Six

Fried Calamari with Mama Nina's Special Sauce

Mixed Green Salad with Creamy Basil Dressing

Bucatini Al'Amatriciana

Lamb Chops Calabrian

Torta Della Nonna

WINES:

With the Calamari—Vichon Chevrignon, 1983

With the Bucatini and Lamb—Rutherford Hill Merlot, 1981

With the Torta—Robert Pecota Muscato De Andrea

Lee Kline and Allen Mc Kay, Owners

Allen Mc Kay, Chef

Ask any 'local' where to find the best fried Calamari and best homemade pasta in the Napa Valley, and undoubtedly you'll hear Mama Nina's. Situated in a low, rambling building with a lovely vegetable and flower garden behind, Mama Nina's offers a relaxing and friendly atmosphere in which to enjoy Northern Italian cooking.

In 1976, when Allen McKay and Lee Kline opened the restaurant, it was the first "up valley" Italian restaurant and a welcome addition to the growing repertoire of French restaurants. It is Allen and Jennifer McKay who today run the restaurant. Pert, redheaded Jennifer handles the front of the house, while husband and chef Allen happily works in the kitchen. Allen, who has travelled to Bologne, Italy to study under Marcella Hazan and Juliano Bugialli, feels "the best food in Italy is in the countryside." Describing his cooking and his restaurant, he says, "It's more country cooking. It's not formal at all. The food reflects that."

Mama Nina's offers two menus for two styles of dining. The menu served in the dining rooms consists of pasta that is made on the premises daily and served in nearly a dozen different ways, and grilled fresh fish and meats. If you opt for lighter fare or are eating on the run, choose the bar and outdoor patio menu, which includes several salads, wonderfully crunchy Calamari, and small handthrown pizzas with crisp crusts and a changing variety of fresh toppings. The vegetable and herb toppings usually come from the McKay's own garden. In addition, Mama Nina's has a full bar, a refreshing alternative for those who get burned out on the 'wine trail'.

6772 Washington Street
Yountville

FRIED CALAMARI WITH MAMA NINA'S SPECIAL SAUCE

*1½ pounds cleaned squid,
drained well to avoid spattering
Peanut oil or vegetable oil,
2 inches deep in skillet
1 cup all-purpose flour
2 tablespoons paprika*

*1 tablespoon granulated garlic
3-4 tablespoons freshly grated
Parmesan cheese
Lemon wedges
MAMA NINA'S SPECIAL
SAUCE*

1. To clean squid, cut off tentacles just above the eye. Squeeze cut end of tentacles to remove the squid's mouth, which looks like a garbanzo bean. Discard it. Reserve the tentacles. On a flat surface, hold the body of the squid by the tail. Holding the blade of a chef's knife almost flat, scrape along the body from tail to cut end, pressing down to squeeze out entrails, but being careful not to break the skin. Discard entrails. The purple membrane covering the squid can be removed or left on. With the point of the knife, stab the transparent quill which protrudes from the body, and hold it fast. Pull the body away. The quill should remain under the knife. Discard the quill. Cut body into rings ½" to 1" wide. Fry with the tentacles.

2. Heat oil in skillet to 375 degrees.

3. Combine flour, paprika, and garlic in a bowl. Toss squid in flour mixture until well coated. Shake off excess. Fry squid in hot oil until golden brown, about 1 minute.

4. Place squid on a serving platter. Sprinkle lightly with Parmesan cheese. Garnish with lemon wedges. Serve MAMA NINA'S SPECIAL SAUCE on the side for dipping. Serve immediately.

MAMA NINA'S SPECIAL SAUCE

1⅔ cup mayonnaise   *6 cloves garlic, minced*
⅓ cup Sriracha sauce*   *Chili sauce to taste**
4 tablespoons ground chili paste*   *Juice of 2 lemons*

Mix mayonnaise, Sriracha sauce, chili paste, chili sauce, garlic, and lemon juice in a bowl. Serve. NOTE: Mama Nina's Special Sauce is very hot. We suggest adding small amounts of the Chili sauce to start and slowly add more until reaching desired degree of hotness.

*Available in Chinese or Vietnamese food stores.

MIXED GREEN SALAD WITH CREAMY BASIL DRESSING

Mixture of green and red leaf   *½ cucumber, sliced*
lettuce and curly endive,   *into thin rounds*
(enough for 6 salads)   *2-3 ripe tomatoes,*
CREAMY BASIL DRESSING   *cut into wedges*

Toss salad greens with CREAMY BASIL DRESSING in a salad bowl. Do not overdress. Garnish with cucumber slices and tomato wedges.

CREAMY BASIL DRESSING

2 cups fresh basil leaves,*   *3 tablespoon Balsamic vinegar*
firmly packed   *2 large cloves garlic*
¼ cup olive oil*   *⅛ teaspoons dried tarragon*
1 cup mayonnaise   *½ teaspoons dry mustard*
½ cup parsley, washed   *3 green onions with tops, chopped*
and stems removed   *Freshly ground pepper*

Combine basil, olive oil, mayonnaise, parsley, green onions, vinegar, tarragon, mustard, garlic, and ground pepper in a blender or food processor until smooth.

*Pesto sauce may be substituted for the fresh basil and olive oil, if desired.

BUCATINI AL'AMATRICIANA

1 pound pancetta*
   or good quality bacon,
   cut into small pieces
2 large red or yellow onions,
   chopped medium fine
5 tablespoons olive oil
3 cloves garlic, minced
½ cup dry white wine
½ cup chicken stock

2 1-pound cans whole tomatoes
2 red hot peppers, crushed OR
1-3 tsp. crushed red pepper flakes
   Salt and freshly ground pepper
   to taste
1 pound bucatini or perciatelli
   pasta**
   Freshly grated Pecorino
   or Parmesan cheese,
   for garnish

1. Sauté pancetta in a skillet until done but not crisp. Remove pancetta from pan and drain on paper towels. Drain bacon drippings from pan and add olive oil.

2. Sauté onions with olive oil over medium heat until limp, about 10 minutes. Add garlic and pancetta. Cook over low heat for 5 minutes to impart its flavor to the onions. Add wine and cook over medium heat for 10 to 15 minutes. Add chicken stock, tomatoes, red peppers, and salt and pepper; simmer for 30 minutes or up to 1 hour.

3. Cook pasta in boiling water until "al dente". Drain well and transfer to a warm serving bowl. Add sauce and toss. Garnish with grated cheese. Serve in bowls.

Pancetta is Italian bacon. It has a more subtle flavor than American bacon. Substituting domestic bacon for pancetta will give the sauce a smokier character.

**Allen indicated that the Bucatini noodle, which is straw-like in shape, was made for this particular sauce. Bucatini or the smaller-sized Perciatelli can be purchased at Italian specialty stores. If unavailable, substitute any kind of noodle.*

LAMB CHOPS CALABRIAN

2-3 tablespoons butter
2-3 tablespoons olive oil
  1 pound mushrooms, cleaned
    and trimmed
  6 loin or rib lamb chops
    Salt and pepper
    All-purpose flour
    for dredging chops

4 fresh artichoke hearts,
  cooked and quartered OR
1 8-ounce jar artichoke hearts
  in oil, drained
6 Anchovy fillets, rinsed
2 tablespoons capers
  Parsley, for garnish
  Olive oil for frying

1. Heat butter and olive oil in a sauté pan over high heat. Add mushrooms; sauté until browned. Set aside.

2. Pound lamb chops to flatten slightly. Season with salt and pepper. Dredge seasoned lamb chops in flour, shaking off excess.

3. Brown lamb chops in hot olive oil in a large skillet over medium heat until done to taste. Drain chops on paper towels.

4. Add artichoke hearts to mushrooms and quickly warm them over medium-high heat.

5. To serve, place lamb chops on serving plates and pour mushroom mixture on top. Garnish with anchovies, capers, and parsley.

TORTA DELLA NONNA
Grandmother's Cake
CRUST

3½ cups unbleached all-purpose flour   3 large eggs
   1 cup sugar   1 cup unsalted butter,
     Grated zest of 2 lemons   at room temperature
                                    Pinch of salt

1. Toss together flour, sugar, lemon zest, and salt in a bowl. Cut in butter with a pastry blender or two knives used scissor-fashion until mixture resembles coarse crumbs.

2. Add eggs, one at a time; gently toss with a fork until mixed. With hands form dough into a ball.

3. Cover with plastic wrap and refrigerate for 1 hour.

FILLING

8 egg yolks
⅔ cup sugar
   Grated zest of 1 orange or lemon
1 cup heavy (whipping) cream

¾ cup hot milk (almost at a boil)
1 ounce blanched almonds,
   coarsely ground
4 tablespoons confectioners'
   sugar, sifted

1. Whisk together egg yolks, sugar, and orange zest in top of a double boiler. Whisk in heavy cream. Slowly pour in hot milk, whisking constantly. Cook mixture over simmering water, whisking constantly until custard thickens and coats the back of a spoon. Pour custard into a glass bowl. Cool completely, about 30 minutes.

2. To assemble, remove pastry dough from refrigerator. Break off ⅔ of it, reserving ⅓. Knead dough on a lightly floured surface for 2 minutes. Using a well- floured rolling pin, evenly roll dough into a circle approximately 16 inches in diameter and ¼-inch thick. Roll half the circle onto rolling pin; carefully lift the dough off floured surface, and set in 12-inch tart pan; unroll dough to cover pan. Gently ease dough into tart pan, leaving an overlap of ½ to 1 inch beyond edge of pan.

3. Knead remaining pastry on a lightly floured surface for 2 minutes. Roll dough as described above into a circle approximately 12-inches in diameter.

4. Pour cooled custard into tart shell.

5. Place pastry circle on top. Gently press down and seal edges of both pastry layers. Fold edges in and press well to seal. Prick top crust with a fork or knife to make vents.

6. Decorate crust edge with diagonal knife cuts evenly spaced. Chill for 15 minutes.

7. Preheat oven to 375 degrees. Bake for 40 to 45 minutes, or until golden brown. Cool.

    To serve, transfer tart to a large round platter, sprinkle with toasted almonds and confectioners' sugar.

    For variation, prepare filling using 1 vanilla bean, split lengthwise, in place of the orange or lemon zest. Remove vanilla bean after cooking.

Dinner for Six

Fresh Cured Salmon with Lemon-Thyme Vinaigrette

Wild Mushroom and Ginger Soup with Chervil Leaves

Loin of Milk-Fed Veal with Pancetta

Port Wine and Orange Sauce

Frangipan Torte

WINES:

With the Salmon—Duckhorn Sauvignon Blanc, 1983

With the Soup—Monticello Gewurztraminer, 1982

With the Veal—Chateau Bouchaine Carneros Pinot Noir, 1982

With the Torte—Schramsberg Crémant

William Harlan, Peter Stocker, and John Montgomery
Owners

Hale Lake, Executive Chef

Meadowood Resort, secluded in its own valley of 250 wooded acres, offers excellent lodging and world-class amenities in a picturesque, country setting. The hillsides of the property are studded with clusters of suites designed to enhance the natural environment. Guests may enjoy golf, swimming, tennis, natural hiking trails, health spa facilities, and, of course, excellent wine-country cuisine. Meadowood is a common oasis for neighboring vintners, since it serves as the home to the Napa Valley Vintners and hosts the prestigious, annual Napa Valley Wine Auction.

Hale Lake, executive chef at Meadowood since 1981, creates innovative California country cuisine that has earned him a loyal and enthusiastic following. Lake, who was born and raised in the Hawaiian fishing village of Kahuku on Oahu, attributes his expert preparation of fresh fish to his island upbringing. His use of tropical fruits and spices is another unique trademark. Asked to describe his cooking, he says "It's very clean food, with the flavors of each ingredient recognizable. I choose to be in California for the product availability, the fresh ingredients with which to be creative. I feel the less you handle an ingredient, the better the end product. I think it's very simple."

Chef Lake oversees all three restaurants on the property. The Pool Watch Cafe and the Fairway Bar and Grill offer casual indoor and outdoor dining.

Lake's cooking artistry is best sampled in the Starmont Restaurant, nestled in a wooded glen overlooking the lush greens of the Meadowood golf course. Dishes such as Carpaccio with Mango chutney, pickled onions and capers, Fresh Ahi grilled and steamed with young cabbage and California caviar, and Dry Aged New York steak with grilled Maui onions and red wine sauce, are good examples of his style.

With its relaxing country setting and luxurious amenities, Meadowood Resort truly captures the feel and lifestyle of the Napa Valley.

900 Meadowood Lane
St.Helena

FRESH CURED SALMON WITH LEMON-THYME VINAIGRETTE

*2 pounds fresh salmon
  King, Atlantic or Chinook
  center cut*
¼ cup sea salt
*3-4 tablespoons golden caviar,
  for garnish*
*¼ cucumber, sliced very thin,
  for garnish*

½ cup brown sugar
*1 bunch coarsely chopped fresh
  dill*
*2 teaspoons crushed white
  peppercorns*
LEMON-THYME VINAIGRETTE

1. Scale and de-bone salmon, cutting the fish into two pieces, along the line of the backbone. (Ask your fish merchant to do this—just specify "Center Cut".) Do not rinse pieces, just wipe dry with paper towels.

2. Mix sea salt and brown sugar in a small bowl. Rub salmon with mixture.

3. Sprinkle one-third of sea salt mixture and one-third of dill in the bottom of an earthenware dish. Place one piece of salmon, skin side down, in dish. Sprinkle with remaining dill, crushed peppercorns, and one-third of salt mixture. Cover with second piece of salmon, skin side up. Sprinkle remaining salt mixture over salmon.

4. Cover with a sheet of aluminum foil and place a light weight on top. Let the gravlax cure for at least 48 hours in the refrigerator, turning the fish at least twice during that period.

5. To serve, cut salmon free from the skin into very thin slices. Place 2 salmon slices on each plate. Roll another slice into a rosette and place it in between the slices. Spoon a thin stream of LEMON-THYME VINAIGRETTE over the bottom half of the salmon. Garnish with caviar and cucumbers, if desired.

LEMON-THYME VINAIGRETTE

¼ cup plus 2 tablespoons
    virgin olive oil
¼ cup plus 2 tablespoons
    hazelnut oil

1 tablespoon balsamic vinegar
2 teaspoons lemon-thyme,
    chopped with no stems
    Juice of 3 lemons

1. Combine olive oil, hazelnut oil, lemon juice, lemon-thyme, and vinegar in a bowl, blending well.

WILD MUSHROOM AND GINGER SOUP WITH CHERVIL LEAVES

5 sprigs chervil
¾ pound wild mushrooms*
   (such as cêpes, chanterelles,
   or bolitis)
2 tablespoons peanut oil
2 tablespoons butter
2 small garlic cloves, minced

1 tablespoon fresh ginger,
   peeled and grated
2 small shallots, minced
3 cups heavy (whipping) cream
   Salt and cayenne pepper
¼ lemon

1. Remove leaves of chervil from stems to yield 2 to 3 teaspoons of leaves.

2. Sauté minced mushrooms with peanut oil in a skillet over high heat until they have rendered their juices. Add butter, garlic, ginger, and shallots. Salt and pepper to taste. Cook until mushrooms are browned, stirring occasionally.

3. Remove one-half of mushroom mixture and reserve for garnish. Add heavy cream to remaining mushroom mixture.

4. Scrape the bottom of skillet to detach any cooked on juices. Pour mixture into a saucepan. Bring to a boil and boil for 2 minutes. Remove from heat.

5. Pour mushroom mixture into a blender and purée. Pour puréed mushrooms into a saucepan. Thin mixture with water until it is the consistency of thick soup. Season with salt, cayenne pepper, and lemon juice to taste. Bring mixture to a boil and keep warm until ready to serve.

6. Ladle soup into small bowls. Garnish with reserved mushroom mixture in the center of each serving. Sprinkle chervil over soup.

   * 1½ounces (about 1½ cups) dried cêpes, first soaked in warm water for at least half an hour and drained, can be used in place of fresh mushrooms.

LOIN OF MILK-FED VEAL WITH PANCETTA AND BASIL
PORT WINE AND ORANGE SAUCE

1 12-ounce sheet of pancetta*
12 leaves of purple, lemon,
   or green basil
2 pounds loin cut milk-fed veal,
   trimmed and silver skin removed

Freshly ground white pepper
Kitchen string
2 tablespoons olive oil

1. Lay sheet of pancetta on a cutting board and place basil leaves in a line down the center of pancetta.

2. Place loin of veal on top of leaves and season well with white pepper. Roll pancetta jelly roll-fashion, so as to wrap the veal inside of it. Tie meat with kitchen string going left to right with 1½ to 2 inches between each tie.

3. Preheat oven to 350 degrees.

4. Add olive oil and pancetta wrapped veal to a sautépan over high heat. Sear on all sides. Bake for 25 minutes or until medium-rare. (Medium-rare = 135 degrees on a meat thermometer.) Meanwhile make PORT WINE AND ORANGE SAUCE.

5. Remove veal from oven and let stand for 5 minutes. Slice ½-inch slices before removing string to minimize chances of pancetta unrolling. Then carefully remove string.

6. To serve, pour 3 to 4 tablespoons of sauce on a dinner plate. Place veal in pancetta onto sauce. Serve with a colorful assortment of your favorite vegetables.

Any leftover veal can be served cold, "picnic style", with mayonnaise flavored with a little Port wine and Orange Sauce.

*Pancetta is Italian bacon and may be purchased from any good butcher.

PORT WINE AND ORANGE SAUCE

3 cups Port wine
1 cup freshly squeezed orange juice
4 cups strong beef or veal stock

½ cup heavy (whipping) cream
Salt and pepper to taste

1. Reduce port and orange juice by one-half in a saucepan over high heat.

2. Add stock and reduce by one-half, skimming the sauce as necessary to remove impurities.

3. Add heavy cream. Season with salt and pepper to taste.

FRANGIPAN TORTE

⅓ cup sugar
¼ cup plus 2 tablespoons butter
1 egg
1½ cups all-purpose flour
1 pound almond paste
Whipped cream, optional

1 cup butter
4 eggs
½ cup cake flour
3 tablespoons sugar
1 pound fresh fruit*

1. Cream ¼ cup plus 2 tablespoons butter and sugar in a small mixing bowl. Add egg. Stir in flour, mixing only until incorporated. With hands, shape dough into a ball. Wrap in plastic and refrigerate until ready to use.

2. Blend almond paste and sugar in a large mixing bowl until smooth. Add 1 cup butter; mix well. Add eggs, one at a time, blending well after each addition. Add flour; mixing only until incorporated. Set aside.

3. Preheat oven to 350 degrees. Dust chilled dough lightly with flour. Slightly flatten dough with hands on a lightly floured surface. Using a well-floured rolling pin, evenly roll dough from center to edges into a 12-inch circle approximately ¼-inch thick. Roll half the circle onto the rolling pin; carefully lift the dough off floured surface, and set it on an 8-inch cake pan; unroll the dough to cover pan (dough should overlap the sides of the pan by about ½-inch). Prick dough ½-inch apart on bottom and sides with a fork.

4. Spread frangipan filling about ½-inch deep in prepared crust. Top filling with a layer of fruit. Continue alternating layers of frangipan and fruit, finishing with a top layer of fruit. Arrange top layer of fruit in an attractive design. Flute edges of dough, or fold them under and press with the tines of a fork to decorate. Bake for 40 to 45 minutes, or until golden.

5. Cool completely. Serve at room temperature. Garnish with whipped cream and berries, if desired.

The torte may be stored for several days in the refrigerator.

*An assortment of raspberries, sliced strawberries, blueberries, and sliced peaches is nice and colorful.

Miramonte Restaurant
and Country Inn

Dinner for Six

Aubergine Provençale

Soupe de Poisson

*L'Agneau au Yogurt
Sauce Cabernet*

Crème Brûlée

WINES:

With the Aubergine—Frog's Leap Sauvignon Blanc, 1984

With the Soupe—Burgess Chardonnay, 1982

With L'Agneau—Inglenook Limited Cask Cabernet Sauvignon, 1980

*With Crème Brûlée—Robert Mondavi Botrytis Late Harvest
Johannisberg Riesling, 1981*

Udo Nechutnys and Edouard Platel, Owners

Udo Nechutnys, Chef

On a back street across from the railroad tracks in St. Helena, is the Miramonte Restaurant and Country Inn, clearly one of the best restaurants in Northern California. When the Miramonte opened in 1979, it was the only restaurant of its caliber in existence in the Napa Valley except for Domaine Chandon. Miramonte was instrumental in putting the Napa Valley on the culinary map, and today the Valley still counts it as one of its best. In fact, many local chefs prefer to have Udo's cooking when they go out to dinner, a true testimonial to his talent.

Miramonte is owned by Udo Nechutnys and Edouard Platel. Platel, a Swiss-born gentleman who sees to the front of the house, says of their philosophy at Miramonte, "We began the restaurant with a dedication to presenting "bonne cuisine",cuisine that is creative and innovative with a keen attention to detail. We have never compromised that over the years."

German-born Udo Nechutnys is the master in the kitchen and consistently turns out dishes bordering on perfection. He draws on his innate talent with food as well as his broad training. He apprenticed in France under mentor, Paul Bocuse. As Udo puts it, "He pushed me to do something and to get confidence in myself." Bocuse encouraged Udo to take a job at the Osaka Hotel School in Japan at the young age of 26. This experience explains the Oriental influence in his cooking today, for he has a respect for fish and vegetables uncommon to most Western chefs, as well as a great talent for beautiful visual presentation.

"Two of the best things in life are wine and food, and then classical music", says the sensitive Nefchutnys. "At Miramonte, we want to please people who want to be spoiled. I want to teach them about the good life through a good meal."And so he does, with a great talent and dedication to perfection that in today's fast paced world, is a rare delight.

1327 Railroad Avenue
St. Helena

AUBERGINE PROVENÇALE
Chinese Eggplant Provence-Style

8 Chinese eggplants,
  unpeeled*
⅓ cup Xeres sherry vinegar
1 cup virgin olive oil**
1 egg yolk
  Oregano, parsley, and thyme
  to taste
½ head of garlic,
  cloves peeled

Salt and pepper to taste
1 fresh tomato,
  peeled and seeded
2 oil-packed sundried tomatoes,
  finely chopped
1 shallot, finely diced
1 bunch of watercress
1 5-inch piece of fresh horseradish,
  finely julienned

1. Steam eggplants until tender. Place warm eggplants in a bowl and pour vinegar over top. Set aside.

2. When the eggplants have cooled and marinated, chop two of them roughly with skin on. (If eggplants appear thick and tough, peel them.)

3. Drain the remaining eggplants, saving vinegar.

4. To prepare the sauce, combine chopped eggplants, olive oil, egg yolk, oregano, parsley , thyme, garlic, and reserved sherry vinegar in a food processor or blender. Blend until smooth. Season to taste.

5. To serve, slice the 6 remaining eggplants lengthwise. Place sauce in the center of individual serving plates. Arrange two eggplant halves skin side up on top of dressing. Artfully arrange garnishes of tomatoes, shallots, watercress, and horseradish around the plate.

Vinegar is wonderful for preserving color in some vegetables. In addition to eggplant, try using vinegar to retain the beautiful color of cooked red cabbage. Pour over and toss, or add to the water you use to steam it.

*You can substitute Japanese or American varieties of eggplant for the Chinese; use 4 small American eggplants, peeled, if the skins are thick.

**Udo prefers the fragrant and fruity olive oil from the Napa Valley Olive Oil Manufacturing Co. in St. Helena.

SOUPE DE POISSON

1 onion, cut into small dice
3 leeks, white part only,
*   cut into small dice*
1 carrot, cut into small dice
½ rib of celery, cut into small dice
3 cloves garlic, minced
1 tablespoon all-purpose flour
3 pounds fresh boneless fish
*   such as rock cod, or fish of your*
*   choice, cut into bite-sized pieces*

2 ripe tomatoes,
*   unpeeled and roughly chopped*
1 tablespoon tomato paste
2½ cups dry white wine
3¼ cup fish stock
*   Dash of Ricard or Pernod liqueur*
*   Saffron to taste*
*   Salt and white pepper to taste*
*   ROUILLE*

1. Sauté onion, leeks, carrot, celery, and garlic in olive oil over low heat, allowing them to "sweat", softening without browning.

2. Sprinkle flour over vegetables, stirring until coated.

3. Add fish, tomatoes, and tomato paste, tossing gently. Add saffron, Ricard, white wine, and fish stock. Season with salt and pepper to taste. Cook uncovered over medium heat for 15 to 20 minutes. Remove from heat.

4. Pour mixture into a blender. Blend briefly. (If desired, reserve some pieces of the fish and reincorporate them before serving.)

5. Strain mixture into a soup pot, pressing hard on any remaining solids.

6. Keep warm until ready to serve. Serve soup with a toasted crouton floating on top of the soup and with a dollop of ROUILLE on top of the crouton.

This soup recipe comes from the father of a friend of Udo. It is a Mediterranean style soup and with the addition of more fish, can easily be served as a main course.

The degree of thickness depends on how much flour you add after sweating vegetables.

ROUILLE

½ baguette, thinly sliced
1 egg yolk
2 cloves garlic, finely minced

½ cup olive oil
Dash of cayenne pepper
Salt and white pepper to taste

1. Toast baguette slices under broiler until light brown.

2. Whisk the egg yolk with the garlic in a small bowl. Slowly add the olive oil to egg yolk mixture, whisking constantly until thick. Make sure the oil becomes emulsified into the sauce before adding more. The sauce should be an extra thick, mayonnaise-like consistency.

3. Season to taste with cayenne, salt and white pepper.

You may wish to pass more croutons and more sauce separately. The ROUILLE is traditionally passed separately and stirred into the fish soup to each person's liking.

L'AGNEAU AU YOGURT DANS LA SAUCE AU CABERNET
Rack of Lamb in Yogurt with Cabernet Sauce

4 cups LAMB STOCK
3 racks of lamb, cleaned
   Salt and pepper
3 shallots, minced
½ cup butter
½ bottle Cabernet Sauvignon
   (375 ml.) good quality
   Parsley, thyme, and oregano,*
   finely chopped, to taste
1 pound mild yogurt,
   such as Pavel

1 pound green beans OR
   3 bunches spinach,
   washed well
2 tablespoons butter
1 cucumber, peeled, seeded,
   and thinly sliced
   Handful of mint leaves,
   julienned
1 bunch green onions,
   finely chopped
1 tomato, peeled, seeded,
   and diced

1. Prepare the LAMB STOCK.

2. Preheat hot oven (450-500). Season racks with salt and pepper. Place a large oven-proof pan over high heat. Add the racks of lamb, turning so all sides are sealed. Roast in oven for 15 minutes, or until meat thermometer reaches 145 degrees. Remove lamb from oven and allow meat to rest for 10 to 15 minutes.

3. "Sweat" shallots with 1 tablespoon butter in a saucepan over medium heat. Add LAMB STOCK and cabernet. Reduce liquid by one-half.

4. Add parsley, thyme, and oregano. Whisk 7 tablespoons butter into sauce. Season with salt and pepper to taste.

5. Warm yogurt in a saucepan over low heat. Be careful--the yogurt will break if heated too quickly.

6. Blanch green beans. Drain and coat with 2 tablespoons butter.

7. To serve, make a bed of beans or spinach in the center of individual serving plates. Cut 2 lamb chops per person. Coat them heavily with lamb sauce and place chops on bed of beans or spinach (the lamb sauce should cover the center of the plate). Pour yogurt around chops. Garnish with cucumber spirals arranged in yogurt. Sprinkle fresh mint, green onions, and chopped tomato on top of the yogurt.

The lamb sauce can be made ahead and reheated when you are ready to assemble the dish; however, do not add parsley, thyme, and oregano until the last minute before serving.

For variation, racks of lamb can be marinated for 3 hours at room temperature in a mixture of onion and garlic juice.

Adding too much thyme can produce a bitter flavor. When seasoning the lamb sauce, you may wish to add more butter or a little cream if it tastes too acidic,or a dash of vinegar if it tastes too sweet.

LAMB STOCK

5 pounds lamb bones	1 bunch parsley, with stems left on
1 onion, with skin left on	1 teaspoon black peppercorns
2 carrots	2 tablespoons tomato paste

1. Preheat oven to 500 degrees. Bake lamb bones in a large roasting pan for 45 minutes, or until well browned.

2. Place bones in a large stock pot. Add onion, carrot, parsley, peppercorns, and tomato paste. Cover with water and simmer for 6 hours. Strain.

Stock can be made ahead and reheated when ready to prepare dish.

CREME BRULEE

3 cups heavy (whipping) cream
1 cup milk
½ vanilla bean, split lengthwise
1 piece of lemon zest

⅓ cup sugar
4 egg yolks
Brown sugar

1. Heat heavy cream, milk, vanilla bean, and lemon zest in a saucepan over medium heat. Bring to a boil. Remove from heat. Remove vanilla bean.

2. Combine sugar and egg yolks in a bowl, stirring until smooth.

3. Slowly add egg mixture to hot milk, stirring constantly. Return mixture to medium heat, stirring constantly until thick enough to coat the back of a spoon. Do not boil.

4. Remove from heat. Place saucepan into ice water to stop cooking process.

5. Preheat oven to 300 degrees.

6. Pour cream mixture into 6 shallow, ovenproof serving dishes. Bake for 18 minutes, or until lightly browned and thickened. Remove from the oven and cool.

7. Sprinkle brown sugar over each serving. Place dishes under broiler until sugar caramelizes. Refrigerate until ready to serve. Serve at room temperature.

MOUNT VIEW HOTEL

Dinner for Six

Monkfish with Red Bell Pepper Sauce

Pineapple Sorbet

Roast Sirloin Strip of Beef with Green Peppercorn Sauce

Almond Pear Tart

WINES:

With the Monkfish—Sterling Vineyards Sauvignon Blanc, 1984

With the Sirloin—Duckhorn Merlot, 1982

With the Tart—Newlan Late Harvest Johannisberg Riesling, 1982

Scott Ullrich, General Manager

Diane Pariseau, Chef

The Mount View Hotel, a two-story beige stucco building with slate blue and burgundy trim, sits proudly over the main street of Calistoga. Built in 1917 by Italian founder Johnny Ghisolfo, the hotel is now owned by Canadians Robert R. McNair and Michael Reimann who, in 1979, completely renovated and restored it to its original Art Deco form.

Several of the hotel suites are named after prominent Calistoga figures and actors popular of the era. Each suite is uniquely decorated according to the tastes of the noted personality. The full-service hotel offers a wide range of events to its guests, from Sunday brunch and special Vintner dinners to afternoon Swing and Dixieland Jazz. Guests may also take advantage of Calistoga's many spa facilities.

Just off the comfortable lobby is Fender's, the hotel's classic Deco lounge. Decorated in jet black and chrome, with original Louis Icart prints on the walls and a polished black Steinway as a focal point, Fender's comes to life with nightly entertainment. Across the lobby from Fender's is the dining room, decorated in a subdued Deco theme, its walls covered with a variety of 1930's framed magazine advertisements that add interest to the simple elegance of the room.

Chef Diane Pariseau presides in the kitchen, creating what she calls "wine country cuisine", a cuisine that focuses strongly on the fresh local products she carefully seeks out. Each evening, in addition to the main menu, Diane creates a four course prix fixe dinner. An abundance of herbs from the garden might stimulate the creation of Baked Double Breast of Chicken with a fresh sage, white wine cream sauce, or Poached Scallops napped with lemon-thyme butter. "I try to create dishes that compliment Napa Valley's fine wines."

1457 Lincoln Avenue
Calistoga

MONKFISH WITH RED BELL PEPPER SAUCE

1½ pounds monkfish
   cleaned of membrane
   Salt, white pepper
   and cayenne pepper to taste
   All-purpose flour
½ cup clarified butter

½ medium onion, medium dice
1 red bell pepper, medium dice
1 cup dry white wine
3 cups heavy (whipping) cream
12 sprigs of chives

1. Cut monkfish into 12 2-ounce portions. Season fish with salt and white pepper. Lightly dust fish with flour just before sautéing. Shake off excess flour.

2. Heat ¼ cup clarified butter over high heat in a large skillet. Add fish and sauté for 2 to 3 minutes on each side until fish becomes firm and light brown. Remove fish from pan and keep warm while preparing sauce.

3. Sauté onions in remaining ¼ cup of clarified butter until translucent. Add red bell pepper and continue sautéing another 4 minutes. Deglaze pan with white wine and reduce liquid by one-half. Add heavy cream and reduce liquid by one-half again. Pour mixture into a blender and purée. Strain to remove any bits that did not purée. Season to taste with salt, white pepper, and cayenne pepper. Keep sauce warm until ready to serve.

4. To serve, spread sauce on 6 plates; place 2 medallions of monkfish on top of sauce. Garnish with chives.

PINEAPPLE SORBET

½ pineapple, peeled and puréed in blender.
   SIMPLE SYRUP

SIMPLE SYRUP

1 cup water   1 sprig rosemary (optional)
2 cups sugar

1. Bring water, sugar, and rosemary to a boil in a saucepan over medium-high heat. Cool. Remove rosemary.

2. Sieve pineapple purée if it is not smooth. Add enough of the simple syrup to pineapple purée to achieve desired level of sweetness.*

3. Transfer mixture into ice cream canister. Prepare according to freezer's directions.

This sorbet can be prepared with the fruit of your choice. Simply adjust the amount of simple syrup depending on the natural sweetness of the fruit.

The purpose of the sorbet is to refresh the palate between courses, so keep the sorbet on the tart side. If making the sorbet for dessert, add more of the simple syrup, if desired.

ROAST SIRLOIN STRIP OF BEEF
WITH GREEN PEPPERCORN SAUCE

4 pounds sirloin strip roast   *Salt*
  GREEN PEPPERCORN SAUCE   *freshly ground black pepper*

1. Preheat oven to 550 degrees. Season roast with salt and pepper. Place in oven and sear for 10 minutes. This seals the outside of the meat and will make for a juicier finished product.

2. Reduce oven temperature to 350 degrees and bake until meat thermometer reaches 120 degrees, (medium-rare) about 40 minutes. Prepare sauce while meat is roasting.

3. When roast is done to your liking, remove from oven and allow to rest for 10 to 15 minutes.

4. To serve, cut two slices per person and arrange on serving plates. Pour prepared sauce over bottom half of slices. Do not cover meat entirely. Serve with roasted baby red potatoes and a seasonal vegetable.

GREEN PEPPERCORN SAUCE

2 shallots, finely diced
3 tablespoons unsalted butter
¾ cup brandy
1 cup beef demi-glace*,
   preferably homemade

1-2 tablespoons green peppercorns
1 cup heavy (whipping) cream
Salt and pepper to taste

1. Sauté shallots in butter without allowing them to brown in a sauté pan over medium heat.

2. Deglaze the pan with brandy and reduce. BE CAREFUL, as brandy may flame.

3. Add demi-glace and reduce by one-third to one-half over high heat until sauce coats the back of a spoon.

4. Add heavy cream and reduce again until sauce is the consistency of very heavy cream.

5. Add green peppercorns to taste just before serving. (Green peppercorns, if cooked too long, can give off a bitter taste.)

6. Season with salt and pepper.

*Demi-glace can be purchased in some gourmet shops.

ALMOND PEAR TART
CRUST

1 cup all-purpose flour
¼ teaspoon salt
½ cup butter

1 3-ounce package cream cheese
Cold water

1. Toss together flour and salt. Cut in butter and cream cheese with a pastry blender or two knives used scissor-fashion until mixture resembles coarse crumbs.

2. Sprinkle cold water, one tablespoon at a time, if needed to bring dough together; gently toss with a fork. With hands form dough into a ball. Cover and refrigerate at least 15 minutes before rolling out.

3. Slightly flatten ball with hands on a lightly floured surface. Using a well-floured rolling pin, evenly roll dough into a circle approximately 11-inches in diameter. Gently ease dough into a 10-inch tart pan. Cover and chill while preparing FILLING.

FILLING

¼ cup butter
⅓ cup sugar
1 egg
¾ cup ground almonds

1½ teaspoons orange flower water
2 ripe pears
½ cup sliced almonds
Whipped cream, for garnish

1. Cream butter and sugar in a mixing bowl until light. Add egg, ground almonds, and orange flower water. Spread filling in tart shell.

2. Position oven rack to low shelf. Preheat oven to 400 degrees.

3. Peel, core, and quarter pears; slice thinly. Arrange pears on top of the filling by starting from the center of the tart and radiating out to the edge,overlapping the pear slices. When finished tart is cut, each serving will have its own row of overlapping slices. Sprinkle slice almonds on top.

4. Bake for 30 minutes, or until top is golden. Serve with whipped cream, if desired.

Dinner for Six

Cornmeal Pancake with Caviar and Crème Fraîche

Grilled Rabbit with Tomato Chipotle Salsa and Black Beans

Grilled Sweet Corn

Garden Tomato Salad

Vanilla Ice Cream with Fresh Berries

WINES:

With the Cornmeal Pancake—Trefethen Chardonnay, 1983

With the Rabbit—Sterling Vineyards Merlot, 1982

Bill Higgins, Cindy Pawlcyn, and Bill Upson, Owners

Cindy Pawlcyn, Chef

S ay "Mustards Grill" to most Napa Valley residents and you'll conjure up mouth-watering thoughts of fun-filled noons and evenings spent in the Valley's most popular casual restaurant. Mustards is a place to see and be seen, an unpretentious place to relax and laugh with friends, a place to try a variety of the best local wines, and most importantly, a place to dine on wonderful food.

Enter Chef Cindy Pawlcyn, a diminutive, creative dynamo who admits to "doing everything passionately." Her passion for cooking, exemplified through the inventive interpretations of simply smoked and grilled fish and meats, local produce, and an everchanging selection of homemade condiments, has won over the hearts (and stomachs) of many locals and visitors.

Cindy is a human tornado full of ideas, which explains the blackboard of daily specials. Says Cindy, " I buy things for the kitchen and then I play with them. I don't like to do the same thing twice in one week." Her personal collection of over 3000 cookbooks, some of which she has had to have translated into English, are one source of her ideas. The others come from an innate feel for what tastes good.

When Mustards opened in 1983, it filled a long-standing dining void. Says owner Bill Higgins, a mischievous looking fellow with a ready, broad smile and an ever-present twinkle in his eye, "The Valley needed a moderately priced American food place where locals could have fun and hang out. AND it needed Cindy Pawlcyn's food." Locals certainly do hang out at Mustards and some vintners have adopted the restaurant as a second home.

Understandable, for it is indeed hard to stay away from tasty whole heads of roasted garlic that spread like butter on crusty, toasted French bread, or flawlessly grilled fresh Sturgeon, or Smoked Sonoma Rabbit with Black Beans, or pencil-thin Onion Rings, or an interpretation of rich, crunchy Strawberry Shortcake that would make you want to write home to Mom.

7399 St. Helena Highway
Yountville

CORNMEAL PANCAKE WITH CAVIAR AND CREME FRAICHE

9 eggs
3 cups milk
⅓ cup yellow cornmeal
⅔ cup white flour
  Pinch of flour
3 tablespoons olive oil
3 tablespoons Brandy

4 tablespoons minced red onions
CREME FRAICHE
2 ounces Beluga or Sevruga caviar
  or Flying Fish roe
  (or as much that is affordable)
2 tablespoons minced chives
  (and chive blossoms if available)

1. For crêpes, beat together eggs, milk, cornmeal, white flour, olive oil, and brandy in a large bowl. Let batter rest for 1 hour. When making crêpes, be sure to stir batter between each crêpe to prevent cornmeal from settling.

2. Heat an 8-inch non-stick pan, and pour about 2 tablespoons batter onto it. Quickly turn pan to spread batter evenly and thinly over the bottom surface. When crêpe batter no longer bubbles and the edges have turned brown, remove crêpe to a plate for stacking additional crêpes.

   You may wish to make all the batter into crêpes (they keep well frozen if tightly wrapped) or hold remaining batter covered in your refrigerator. Batter will keep for almost a week.

3. Preheat oven to 450 degrees. Place one crêpe in individual gratin dishes or on small ovenproof plates. Top each crêpe with 2 teaspoons red onion and 2 tablespoons Crème Fraîche. Fold crêpe in half and sprinkle a few more chopped onions next to the fold.

4. Bake for 8 minutes, or until warm and bubbly. Remove from oven.

5. Top with a dollop of Crème Fraîche. Garnish with caviar and chives.

CREME FRAICHE

1 cup heavy (whipping) cream   ¼ cup buttermilk

1. Combine heavy cream and buttermilk. Let mixture sit at room temperature for 12 to 18 hours.

2. Refrigerate until ready to use.

GRILLED RABBIT WITH TOMATO CHIPOTLE SALSA
AND BLACK BEANS

3 rabbits, 2½-3 pounds each
1 teaspoon cayenne pepper
10 cloves garlic, peeled and minced
    Zest of 1 orange
    Juice of 1 orange
1 4-ounce tin of chipotle chilies
    in adobo* (not in vinegar)

¼ cup good quality sherry vinegar
    Pinch of salt
2 tablespoons olive oil
2 tablespoons cilantro sprigs,
    for garnish
SALSA

1. Remove front and hind legs of rabbits. De-bone thighs. Remove loins from backbone on both sides. Place rabbit pieces in a shallow pan.

2. Mix together cayenne pepper, garlic, orange zest, orange juice, 2 ounces chilies (reserve remaining 2 ounces for SALSA), sherry vinegar, salt, and olive oil in a bowl. Pour mixture over rabbit pieces. Cover and refrigerate for 3 hours or overnight. Remove marinated rabbit pieces and dry. Save marinade for basting rabbit and sauce.

3. Prepare a medium-hot grill. Roast rabbit slowly, about 20 to 25 minutes. Turn frequently and baste with marinade.

4. Serve one-half of a rabbit per person, arranging pieces on warm serving plates. Serve SALSA on the side. Garnish with cilantro. Serve with BLACK BEANS.

SALSA

Remaining chipotle marinade
Remaining half of the 4-ounce tin
of chipotle chilies
1 medium onion, diced
5 cloves garlic, minced
2 tablespoons minced cilantro
2 tablespoons olive oil

2 medium tomatoes, peeled,
seeded, and diced
Juice of 1 orange
Zest of 1 orange
2 ounces toasted almonds,
chopped
½ cup veal or chicken stock

1. Combine reserved marinade with remaining 2 ounces chipotle chilies in a blender; strain.

2. Sauté onion and garlic with oil in a skillet over medium heat. Add tomatoes, orange zest, and orange juice; allow liquid to reduce a little. Add chipotle mixture, almonds, and stock. Cook until thick. Stir in Cilantro.

*Chipotle chilies are jalapeno chilies that are grown until they are red and very ripe. They are then sun-dried and smoked. Adobo is a tomato-based sauce. 1 or 2 fresh jalapeno peppers can be substituted for the chipotle chilies, but the results will be different since Chipotle chilies give a special tangy, smokey flavor to the dish.

NOTE: Chipotle chilies are very hot, so adjust the amount of chilies used in the salsa to taste.

BLACK BEANS

1 pound black beans
4 slices bacon, minced
1 onion, chopped medium fine
2 jalapeno peppers, minced
5 cloves garlic, minced
3 ribs celery, minced
2 carrots, minced
2 bay leaves

Salt and pepper to taste
Cumin to taste
Thyme to taste
1 ham hock
4 cups chicken or veal stock
Sour cream, for garnish
Cilantro, minced, for garnish
Red onion, minced, for garnish

1. Place black beans in a large saucepan filled with boiling water; cook for 5 minutes. Drain beans. Set aside.

2. Cook bacon until golden brown in a large pot over medium-high heat. Add onion, jalapeno peppers, garlic, celery, carrots, bay leaves, salt and pepper, cumin, and thyme. Cook until vegetables are wilted, but not browned. Add ham hock and beans, and cover with stock. Reduce heat to medium-low and simmer until beans are tender.

3. Garnish with sour cream, cilantro, and red onions.

GRILLED SWEET CORN

6 ears sweet corn with husks on,   HERB BUTTER
    preferably just picked
    from the garden*

1. Peel back outer layers of husk and remove silk.

2. Replace outer husk, and place corn on grill for 5-8 minutes, depending on the heat.

3. Rub grilled ears with HERB BUTTER.

(*If corn is not just picked, clean as described above and soak in lightly salted water for 1 hour. Remove from water, allow to drain, and then grill.)

For variation, rub ears with herb butter before replacing husks.

HERB BUTTER

⅓ cup butter,   1 tablespoon finely minced favorite
    at room temperature   fresh herb
                                     (try parsley or basil)

1. Combine butter and herb in a small bowl.

GARDEN TOMATO SALAD

*6 very large ripe tomatoes,
⅓-inch slices*
*1 medium sweet red onion,
peeled and thinly sliced*

2-3 tablespoons minced chives
VINAIGRETTE
Freshly ground white pepper

1. Lay tomato slices down center of oval serving plate, overlapping slightly. Sprinkle onion rings and chives over tomatoes.

2. Drizzle VINAIGRETTE down center of tomatoes. Do not overdress. Top with pepper.

VINAIGRETTE

3 tablespoons champagne vinegar
9 tablespoons extra virgin olive oil
*3 shallots, minced
  (or 2 green onions minced)*

1 tablespoon Dijon mustard
Salt and white pepper to taste

1. Combine Champagne vinegar, olive oil, shallots, mustard, and salt and pepper; mix well.

Yield: ¾ cup

VANILLA ICE CREAM

2 cups extra rich milk*
1 teaspoon vanilla extract
¾ cup sugar
1 cup heavy (whipping) cream

½ vanilla bean, split lengthwise
   and scraped of seeds
6 large egg yolks
   Pinch of salt

1. Combine milk, vanilla, ¼ cup plus 2 tablespoons sugar, split vanilla bean, and scrapings from vanilla bean in a saucepan over low heat; scald milk.

2. Beat egg yolks with remaining sugar in a bowl until thick and light. Slowly beat in milk mixture. Remove vanilla bean and re- scrape pod to remove all flavor; discard. Return milk mixture to medium heat and cook, stirring constantly, until mixture coats the back of a spoon. Cool.

3. Beat whipping cream and salt in a chilled bowl with chilled beaters until soft peaks form. Fold whipped cream into custard. Transfer mixture into ice cream canister. Prepare according to freezer's directions.

4. Serve with ripe berries or peaches tossed with granulated sugar and kirsch, if desired.

Yield: 1 quart

Extra rich milk can be found in some supermarkets. It is whole milk with additional butterfat. If unavailable, use whole milk.

THE ST.GEORGE RESTAURANT

Dinner for Six

Aegean Pasta

Mediterranean Spinach Salad

Pollo San Giorgio

Pashka

WINES:

With the Pasta—Grgich Hills Sauvignon Blanc, 1983

With the Chicken—Freemark Abbey "Bosche"
Cabernet Sauvignon, 1977

With the Pashka—Hans Kornell Cellars Brut Champagne

Newton Cope, Owner

Paul Wiggins, Chef

S ituated just over the railroad tracks in St. Helena is the St. George Restaurant, a large, windowless, brick building surrounded by a high, brick, courtyard wall. Sound foreboding? Don't be put off by the exterior, for inside the wall is a lovely expansive brick patio where, in good weather, patrons may relax and dine. The patio courtyard is studded with fruitless Mulberry trees encased in planters. In one corner away from the restaurant itself, is an old, vine-covered, stone building that was used for Sherry storage back in the 1880's. The owners wisely preserved it, and it now houses a beautifully decorated bar.

Inside the high-ceilinged St. George, the feeling is one of a large Victorian drawing room, only with a European flavor created by the larger-than-life paintings and unusual antiques that owner Newton Cope loves to collect and share with his patrons. One of the most interesting paintings is one he recently commissioned artist Michael Keating to paint of Napa Valley vintners. The painting depicts a scene on the restaurant's patio of a gathering of local wine personalities, some of whom you are bound to recognize, as the likenesses are quite good.

The cuisine at the St. George is Continental with strong Mediterranean overtones. Says Chef, Paul Wiggins, "We emphasize fresh seafood and homemade pasta. We even do our own smoking of meats and fish on the premises." Paul is American-born but spent his childhood living abroad with his family. Living in Belgium in his late teens, he discovered his love for cooking and began his career in the world of food. The menu he has selected is very representative of the St. George's own menu.

1050 Charter Oak
St. Helena

AEGEAN PASTA

⅓ cup olive oil
1 tablespoon chopped garlic
1 cup fresh tomatoes,
   peeled, seeded, and diced
3 tablespoons chopped parsley
2 teaspoons oregano

¼ cup calamata olives,
   pitted and chopped
1 pound fresh baby shrimp
2 tablespoons butter
¾ pound fresh linguine (dry weight),
   cooked al-dente

1. Heat olive oil in a large sauté pan over medium-high heat until it almost smokes. Add garlic, tomatoes, parsley, olives, and oregano. Cook until bubbling.

2. Add shrimp, cooking until they just turn pink. Stir in butter until melted.

3. Toss shrimp mixture and pasta in a large serving bowl. Serve immediately.

Cooking the sauce for this dish takes very little time, so have pasta cooked or nearly cooked when you begin the sauce.

MEDITERRANEAN SPINACH SALAD

2 bunches fresh spinach,
   leaves washed and dried
   stems removed
1 small red onion,
   sliced into thin rings to taste
1 pound Greek Feta cheese

1 cup extra virgin olive oil
⅓ cup red wine vinegar
Salt and freshly cracked black
pepper

Calamata olives, for garnish*

1. Combine spinach leaves, red onion, and Feta cheese in a salad bowl. Set aside.

2. Blend olive oil, vinegar, and salt and pepper in a small bowl.

3. Toss salad with dressing, taking care not to bruise the spinach leaves. Serve on chilled salad plates. Garnish with olives.

   *Calamata olives, a type of Greek olive, may be purchased at specialty shops, or at Greek or Italian markets.

POLLO SAN GIORGIO

1 ounce Porcini mushrooms, dried
6 whole chicken breasts, boned
  Salt and pepper
¼ cup chopped parsley
6 thin slices proscuitto ham

1 pound Asiago cheese, crumbled
¼ cup chopped shallots
2 cups Marsala wine
6 cups heavy (whipping) cream
3 tablespoons olive oil

1. Soak mushroom, covering completely in water. Set aside.

2. Lay chicken breasts, skin side down, on a work table. Sprinkle salt and pepper, and parsley over each breast. Place a slice of proscuitto on each breast.

3. Divide crumbled Asiago cheese into six portions. Press each portion with hands until it congeals; place on top of proscuitto, Wrap edges of chicken breast around cheese, folding the skin toward the center of breast. Turn chicken "packets" over, skin side up; set aside. (NOTE: The chicken breasts can be made ahead of time up to this point and refrigerated.)

4. Combine shallots and Marsala wine in a heavy 3 to 4 quart saucepan over medium heat. Reduce liquid to ½ cup. Add heavy cream and reduce to 2 cups.

5. Drain mushrooms. Add mushrooms to cream sauce, reserving some for garnish, if desired. Keep sauce warm over low heat.

6. Preheat oven to 450 degrees. Cook chicken, fold side down, in olive oil in a heavy, oven-proof sauté pan over high heat for 2 to 3 minutes without turning. Transfer sauté pan to oven. Roast for 15 to 25 minutes, depending on size of chicken breasts.

7. To serve, arrange your favorite rice on serving plates; top with chicken breasts. Pour warm sauce over top. Garnish with reserved mushrooms, if desired.

PASHKA

2 8-ounce packages cream cheese,
  softened
¾ pound unsalted butter,
  at room temperature
1¼ cups confectioners' sugar

1 tablespoon vanilla
1½ cups currants
1½ cups toasted almonds
MELBA SAUCE
ladyfingers (optional)

1. Beat cream cheese and butter in a mixing bowl until smooth, about 5 to 10 minutes. Add sugar and vanilla; mix well.

2. Stir in currants and almonds. Cover and refrigerate for at least 2 to 4 hours, or overnight.

3. To serve, scoop Pashka into individual dessert dishes. Top with MELBA SAUCE. Garnish with lady fingers or favorite cookie, if desired.

MELBA SAUCE

1 cup raspberries, fresh
  or frozen

Granulated sugar, to taste
Dash of raspberry liqueur, optional

1. In a saucepan, heat raspberries until almost boiling.

2. Add sugar to taste. If desired, flavor with raspberry liqueur. Chill until ready to use.

Yield: 1 scant cup
Pashka will keep in the refrigerator covered for about a week.

SILVERADO

Dinner for Four

Wilted Wisconsin Duck Salad

Medallions of Veal and Prawns

Chocolate Decadence Cake

WINES:

With the Salad—Robert Mondavi Johannisberg Riesling, 1984

With the Veal—Beaulieu Sauvignon Blanc, 1983

With the Cake—Beringer Knights Valley Cabernet Sauvignon, 1981

Kirk Candland, General Manager

Emmanuel Afentoulis, Executive Chef

D riving up the long, curved drive to the grand, white mansion at Silverado Country Club feels a little like arriving at Tara. Built in the 1870's by an Indiana Civil War general and U.S. senator, the graceful mansion still grandly sits at the center of the resort's 1200 acres, tucked in among gentle hills, ancient groves, and a boundless maze of Napa vineyards. The resort offers 269 private accommodations, two of the finest golf courses in Northern California, eight swimming pools, and one of the largest and best designed tennis complexes in the West.

Silverado is a home of gracious living with the ambience created by its wide, flowered walkways, palm-studded landscape, and pristine lawns. In the Napa Valley, gracious living always includes fine dining. At the Silverado Country Club, three fine restaurants provide a variety of dining alternatives. The Royal Oaks is an intimate grill, serving prime beef and fresh seafood. The Bar and Grill, overlooking the North Course, offers casual daytime dining to golfers. The most elegant dining room at Silverado is the Vintner's Court, serving "New American" cuisine mixed with a touch of French continental. The Vintner's Court offers an exclusive all Napa Valley wine list. The Friday evening Seafood Buffet and Sunday brunch are food extravaganzas not to be missed.

Overseeing all food operations on the property is Executive Chef, Emmanuel Afentoulis. · The Greek-born chef runs four kitchens, and believes, that to keep this large operation running well, it is necessary to share his knowledge and develop his sous chefs. "To fulfill your profession is to give to people within the profession", says Afentoulis.

Chef Afentoulis shares some favorite recipes from the Vintner's court in the following menu.

1600 Atlas Peak Road
Napa

WILTED WISCONSIN DUCK SALAD

2 tablespoons olive oil
2-3 cloves garlic,
  chopped
½ teaspoon fresh ginger,
  peeled and chopped
4 slices bacon, cooked crisp
  and crumbled
½ cup red wine vinegar*
8 ounces smoked duck,
  cut into slivers

2 bunches watercress,
  cleaned and trimmed
4 leaves radiccio,
  cut into 1 inch squares
¼ cup toasted pine nuts
8 cherry tomatoes,
  cut in half
2 tablespoons toasted sesame seeds
  Salt and pepper to taste
8 lemon wedges

1. Heat olive oil in a large skillet over medium-high heat. Add garlic and sauté until golden. Add ginger, bacon, red wine vinegar, and duck. Cook for 1 minute until hot.

2. Toss together watercress and radiccio in a large mixing bowl. Add hot duck mixture and toss thoroughly. Add pine nuts; toss.

3. Divide salad onto 4 plates. Place tomato halves around salad. Sprinkle sesame seeds on top. Season to taste. Garnish with lemon wedges.

This salad may also be made with smoked pheasant or quail, or with roast duck or chicken.

*For a different flavor, Balsamic vinegar may be substituted for red wine vinegar.

MEDALLIONS OF VEAL AND PRAWNS

½ cup butter
8 2-ounce pieces of boneless
   veal loin, slightly pounded
8 jumbo prawns,
   peeled and deveined
1 cup seasoned flour*

1 shallot, minced
2 tablespoons Madeira
¼ cup chicken stock
1 teaspoon tarragon
2 teaspoons lemon juice
   Salt and pepper to taste
3 tablespoons butter

1. Melt ½ cup butter in a heavy skillet over medium-high heat. Dredge veal and prawns in seasoned flour. Shake off excess. Place in skillet and cook for 2 minutes. Turn and cook for 2 minutes. Transfer veal and prawns to a warm serving plate.

2. Drain excess butter from skillet. Add shallots; cook for 1 minute. Add Madeira, stock, tarragon, lemon juice, and salt and pepper. Bring to a boil and reduce liquid slightly. Blend 3 tablespoons butter into sauce.

3. To serve, place two veal medallions, each topped with a prawn, on individual serving plates. Pour sauce over top. Serve immediately.

*Season all-purpose flour with salt, thyme, oregano, cayenne pepper, or whatever seasonings you prefer.

CHOCOLATE DECADENCE CAKE

*1½ pounds dark (semi-sweet) chocolate,
   coarsely chopped
½ cup plus 2 tablespoons butter
5 eggs, at room temperature
3 tablespoons sugar
3 scant tablespoons all-purpose flour*

*2 tablespoons Grand Marnier
  Strawberry purée*
4 fresh strawberries, for garnish
  Whipped cream, for garnish
4 mint leaves, for garnish*

1. Grease a 9 or 10-inch round cake pan. Preheat oven to 400 degrees. Melt chocolate and butter in a double boiler over simmering water, stirring until smooth. Remove from heat. Set aside.

2. Beat eggs and sugar in a medium mixing bowl until light and fluffy. Sift in flour; stir. Fold egg mixture, ⅓ at a time, into chocolate mixture. Add Grand Marnier, mixing until smooth.

3. Pour batter into prepared pan. Bake for 10 to 12 minutes, or until surface is slightly dry to touch. Turn oven off and leave cake in oven for an additional 10 minutes. Cool completely before serving.

4. To serve, spoon enough strawberry purée to cover bottom of serving plates. Place a small wedge of cake on top. Place a small dollop of whipped cream on cake or 2 dollops on the purée. Garnish with strawberries and mint leaves.

*Strawberry purée is made from fresh or frozen berries, cooked down slightly with a little sugar and strained to remove seeds.

This is a wonderful, very rich and intense chocolate cake, so serve small portions. Like other dense chocolate desserts, Chocolate Decadence freezes well and improves in flavor with a little age. When Chef Afentoulis makes this cake at home, he freezes it for 24 hours, then thaws it and serves.

Make sure to cut Chocolate Decadence cake with a hot knife.

Silverado Restaurant
Creative American Cooking ~ Award Winning Wine List

Dinner for Four

Steamed Mussels with Ginger, Shiitake Mushrooms
and Chinese Fermented Black Beans

Grilled Fresh Pork Loin
with Roasted Tomato and Toasted Chili Peppers

Warm Scallops With Young Greens

Chocolate Macadamia and Caramel Tarte

WINES:

With the Mussels—Girard Chenin Blanc, 1983

With the Pork—Chateau Montelena Zinfandel, 1982

With the Salad—St. Clement Chardonnay, 1983

Alex and Mark Dierkhising, Owners

Mark Dierkhising, Chef

As fate would have it, Mark and Alex Dierkhising apparently had no choice but to be in the restaurant business. Coming from a large restaurant family in Minnesota, all eight children in their family have become involved with food and wine.

Alex, having a strong interest in wine, sought out a restaurant of his own in the Napa Valley. In the mid-seventies, he bought the Silverado Restaurant, and set about creating one of the most extensive wine lists in the United States. He succeeded, for The Wine Spectator has awarded his restaurant's wine list with its Grand Award for the past 4 consecutive years. With over 1200 selections, it is the largest wine list in the Napa Valley.

Brother Mark is the resident chef,and describes his cooking as "creative" American. " We make everything from scratch, even our own jams." Mark, a graduate of the Culinary Institute of America, believes, "Cooking is really a science. You have to understand food chemistry to be able to recreate recipes." He has been fortunate to meet and to work with great foreign chefs, such as Chinese chef and friend, Ken Hom. Cooking in Hong Kong with Hom has strongly influenced his cooking style, and several dishes at Silverado Restaurant are a creative combination of Chinese and Mexican cooking.

The Silverado Restaurant with its casual California redwood decor, serves breakfast, lunch, and dinner to Calistoga locals and tourists. So successful is this operation that they have outgrown their space and have opened another business, All Seasons Market, across the street. A combination restaurant, market, and wine shop, it offers a variety of fresh fish, meats, cheeses, and ready-to-go gourmet dishes. A huge selection of wine is available, to be taken out or drunk in the restaurant. All Seasons also has regular wine tastings, conducted on a drop-in basis, in its wine room.

1374 Lincoln Avenue
Calistoga

STEAMED MUSSELS WITH GINGER, SHIITAKE MUSHROOMS AND CHINESE FERMENTED BLACK BEANS

24 preserved Chinese black beans*
4 tablespoons unsalted butter
1 tablespoon minced shallots
1 teaspoon minced garlic
2 thin slices of fresh ginger
48 mussels, with beards removed

1 cup dry white wine,
   preferably dry Chenin Blanc
   or Sauvignon Blanc
8 fresh Shiitake mushrooms,
   diced*

1. Soak black beans in water to remove some of the salt; drain.

2. Place butter, shallots, garlic, and ginger in a saucepan with a lid over medium heat. Sweat mixture until transparent. Add mussels and white wine. Increase heat to high and cook until mussels just open, removing mussels from pan as they open to a bowl kept in a warm place. Discard any unopened mussels. Add mushrooms and black beans. Reduce mixture until sauce becomes thick.

3. To serve, arrange mussels on 4 serving plates. Pour sauce over mussels.

*Available at most Oriental grocery stores. The Shiitake mushrooms, if unavailable, can be omitted and dried black Chinese mushrooms substituted. Do, however, reconstitute them in some water before using.

SILVERADO RESTAURANT

GRILLED FRESH PORK WITH ROASTED TOMATO
AND TOASTED CHILI PEPPERS

2 pounds pork loin
½ teaspoon cumin
½ teaspoon ground coriander
½ teaspoon freshly ground
* black pepper*
Juice of 1 lemon

⅛ cup olive oil
½ teaspoon salt,
* preferably Kosher*
TOMATO AND PEPPER SAUCE

1. Remove all fat and bluing from pork loin and cut into ½ inch cutlets. Place cutlets between pieces of wax paper or plastic wrap and pound them into scallops to tenderize meat. 15 to 30 minutes before grilling pork, place scallops in marinade.

2. For marinade, combine cumin, coriander, pepper, lemon juice, olive oil, and salt in a small bowl. Pour mixture over pork scallops.

3. Prepare a hot grill. Grill marinated pork scallops to well done or desired tenderness. (For rare pork, freeze loin in advance to less than -11 degrees, to destroy any possible trichinae present.) Be careful not to overcook or burn scallops.

4. To serve, place scallops on a serving platter. Garnish with seasonal fresh vegetables. Pass TOMATO AND PEPPER SAUCE.

TOMATO AND PEPPER SAUCE

4 large ripe tomatoes   *Juice of 1 lime*
2 Pasilla peppers   *2 tablespoon chopped cilantro*
1 Fresno pepper   *Freshly ground pepper to taste*
2 Anaheim peppers   *Kosher salt to taste*

1. Preheat oven to 450 degrees.

2. Remove the stem from the tomatoes and cut an"X" in the bottom of each one. Place tomatoes on a cookie sheet. Roast for 15 minutes. (This will allow for easy removal of the skin and will impart a distinctive flavor.) Set tomatoes aside until cool enough to handle.

3. Place the Pasillas peppers, Fresno peppers, and Anaheim peppers under the broiler until skins char, turning the peppers as they blacken. Be careful not to overcook the flesh of the peppers. When all sides are charred, place peppers into a bowl and cover bowl with plastic wrap. Leave peppers covered for 15-45 minutes, then peel off the skins and remove the seeds. Use rubber gloves if your skin is sensitive. Peeling peppers under cool running water will help in the process, although you will lose some of the flavor this way. Chop peppers coarsely. Set aside.

4. Remove tomato skins. Cut tomatoes in half. Squeeze out seeds and juice, leaving the pulp to be chopped the same size as the chili peppers.

5. Combine tomatoes, peppers, lime juice, cilantro, black pepper and salt. Let mixture sit for a minimum of 1 hour, or up to three days, refrigerated. Serve sauce at room temperature.

Note: The kinds of peppers you use in this recipe can vary according to your preference or availability. Try to select a variety to add complexity to the flavor and for variation in level of hotness.

The Tomato Pepper Sauce and marinade also works well with grilled chicken or game birds. Pork chops can be used in place of the pork loin.

Since this menu would be ideal for a cool, Autumn evening, serve Butternut or Acorn squash, or oven-roasted potatoes and turnips to accompany the Pork loin.

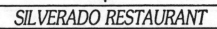

WARM SCALLOPS WITH YOUNG GREENS

1 teaspoon minced shallots
1 teaspoon minced garlic
4 tablespoons olive oil
½ cup white wine
½ pound fresh scallops

¼ cup olive oil (optional)
1 teaspoon Balsamic vinegar
2 tablespoons white wine vinegar
1 teaspoon hazelnut oil (optional)
Enough washed young greens
for 4 salads

1. "Sweat" shallots and garlic with 4 tablespoons olive oil in a sauté pan over low heat until transparent. Add white wine and scallops. Cook scallops until just barely done. Remove scallops from pan; set aside.

2. Reserve liquid in pan and reduce it by one-half. Add ¼ cup olive oil, Balsamic vinegar, white wine vinegar, and hazelnut oil. Toss mixture with scallops. Toss scallops with young greens in a salad bowl. Arrange dressed greens and warm scallops on 4 salad plates. Serve immediately.

This salad can also be used for a main course. Increase the amount of greens and scallops, and serve with a hearty soup and crunchy French bread.

CHOCOLATE MACADAMIA AND CARAMEL TARTE
CRUST

2½ cups all-purpose flour
¼ cup sugar
⅛ teaspoon salt

¾ cup butter, chilled
and cut into small cubes
1 egg

1. Toss together flour, sugar, and salt in a bowl. Cut in butter with a pastry blender or two knives used scissor-fashion until mixture resembles coarse crumbs. Add egg; mix until dough is just moistened. With hands, form dough into a ball. Slightly flatten ball with hands on a lightly floured surface. Using a well-floured rolling pin, evenly roll dough into a circle approximately 10-inches in diameter and ¼-inch thick. Gently ease dough into a 9-inch tart pan. Cover and refrigerate for at least 15 minutes.

2. Preheat oven to 375 degrees. Prick tart shell ½ inch apart over bottom with a fork. Bake for 18 minutes. Cool completely.

FILLING

½ cup sugar
½ cup dark corn syrup
¼ cup butter

1 cup heavy (whipping) cream
2 scant cups Macademia nuts,
unsalted

1. Combine sugar, corn syrup, butter, and ½ cup heavy cream in a small saucepan over medium-low heat, stirring constantly until sugar is dissolved. Continue cooking, stirring constantly, until mixture reaches 244 degrees on a candy thermometer. Remove from heat.

2. Stir in remaining ½ cup heavy cream to hot sugar mixture. Return to heat, and cook, stirring constantly until mixture reaches 230 degrees on a candy thermometer. Pour mixture into a clean bowl. Cool completely.

3. Preheat oven to 375 degrees. Evenly spread macadamia nuts on cookie sheet. Roast for 10 minutes. Halfway through cooking time, rotate pan and stir nuts. Watch carefully during last few minutes to prevent burning. Set aside.

CHOCOLATE TOPPING

¼ cup plus 2 tablespoons
  heavy (whipping) cream
1½ teaspoons light corn syrup
¼ cup sugar

1½ tablespoons butter
3 ounces semi-sweet chocolate,
  coarsely chopped

1. Stir together heavy cream, sugar, corn syrup, and butter in a heavy saucepan over medium-low heat until hot. Remove from heat. Stir in chocolate, blending until melted. Cool.

2. To assemble, reserve a small amount of caramel to make a spiral design on finished tart. Spread remaining caramel carefully into baked tart shell. Coarsely chop roasted Macademia nuts; press them into caramel filling. Spread chocolate glaze over caramel and nut layers. Refrigerate until glaze is set, about 15 minutes.

3. Place reserved caramel into a pastry bag with a small round tip. Starting in middle of tart, pipe out a thin spiral design. With the dull side of a paring knife, draw lines from the center to the edges of the tart, creating a spider-web effect.

4. Serve at room temperature.

This delicious dessert tastes like a rich candy bar, and is worth every calorie for the indulgence!

SPRING·STREET

Dinner for Six

Cabbage Ham Soup

Bakery Lane Frittata

Green Salad with Cumin Dressing

Grape Almond Pie

WINES:

With the Soup—Ehler's Lane Sauvignon Blanc, 1983

With the Frittata—Schug Cellars Carneros Pinot Noir, 1983

Jim and Amanda Zimmer
Alan and Susan Zimmer
Owners

Craig Virgo, Chef

SPRING STREET RESTAURANT

Y ou walk up the front walk to a bungalow that might be found in any small town in America except that here, on a side street in St. Helena, the house is the Spring Street Restaurant. Opened four years ago by two local women with no restaurant experience, Spring Street quickly filled the need for a friendly hometown restaurant catering to local people. What the locals liked was pure and simple home cooking in a relaxed garden setting. Serving lunch and dinner, the menu includes wonderful salads with fabulous dressings, homemade soups and breads, sandwiches, and desserts.

Formerly the home of San Francisco opera singer, Walter Martini, the house is now decorated simply with quilt-covered tables bedecked with small bouquets of fresh flowers. Hardwood floors are throughout,and a large blackboard indicates daily specials. French doors open onto an airy, front porch and adjacent patio where, in good weather, patrons may dine. Nearby, is a large tiled courtyard, lush with a vine-covered trellis and a large stone fountain.

In 1985, Jim and Amanda Zimmer bought Spring Street. They have maintained the style of the restaurant, and expanded service to include dinner and Sunday brunch. Jim is no stranger to the restaurant business, having worked for large restaurant corporations for many years. Finally realizing a dream to operate his own restaurant, he says, " I love every minute of working in the restaurant. We will continue to offer a fresh, reasonably-priced menu with all items homemade on the property."

Jim and Amanda are continuing a recipe exchange program begun by the former owners. Any guest who gives the restaurant a recipe that fits the style and spirit of Spring Street may have one of their recipes. The five secret salad dressing recipes that have been a key to the success of the restaurant cannot be divulged, but other delicious recipes are graciously given. The following menu is representative of Spring Street.

1245 Spring Street
St. Helena

SPRING STREET RESTAURANT

CABBAGE HAM SOUP

¼ cup diced green pepper
¼ cup diced celery
½ cup diced onion
2 tablespoons chopped parsley
3 tablespoons butter
2 cups diced cooked ham

1 bay leaf
2 tablespoons flour
3 cups chicken stock or broth
2 cups finely shredded white cabbage
1 tablespoon water
1 cup sour cream

1. Sauté green pepper, celery, onion, and parsley in 2 tablespoons butter in a soup pot until soft.

2. Add ham and bay leaf. Cook until ham is heated.

3. Blend flour and chicken stock in a bowl; add to ham mixture. Bring to a boil, stirring constantly. Decrease heat to low and simmer.

4. Melt remaining 1 tablespoon butter in a sauté pan. Add cabbage and water. Cook until cabbage turns bright and softens.

5. Add cabbage to stock mixture.

6. Garnish each serving with a spoonful of sour cream.

BAKERY LANE FRITTATA

¾ cup diced green pepper
1½ cups sliced mushrooms
1½ cups diced zucchini
¾ cup chopped onion
1 large clove garlic, minced
3 tablespoons oil
1 teaspoon black pepper,
   freshly ground

¼ cup light cream
1 pound cream cheese, cut
   into ¾-inch cubes*
6 eggs, beaten
1½ cups shredded cheddar cheese
2 cups seasoned croutons,
   preferably homemade**
1 teaspoon salt

1. Butter a 9x13-inch baking pan. Preheat oven to 350 degrees.

2. Sauté green pepper, mushrooms, zucchini, onion, and garlic with oil in a skillet until zucchini is crisp tender. Cool slightly.

3. Beat eggs and light cream in a large bowl. Add cream cheese, cheddar cheese, croutons, salt, pepper, and sautéed vegetables. Mix well.

4. Pour mixture into prepared pan. Bake for 40 minutes , or until set in center. Cool for 10 minutes before serving.

Spring Street recommends hand chopping the vegetables, as opposed to processing in a food processor,to give a nice chunky texture to the frittata.

* To facilitate cutting the cream cheese into cubes, place cream cheese in the freezer for 10-15 minutes to solidify it prior to cutting.

**Seasoned croutons may be purchased in any grocery store. To make homemade croutons, toss day old bread cubes in melted butter with fresh or dried herbs, garlic, and pepper. Do not saturate with butter. Toast until evenly browned under broiler, turning croutons often.

GREEN SALAD WITH CUMIN DRESSING
CUMIN DRESSING

¼ cup sour cream
¼ cup mayonnaise
⅛ teaspoon garlic powder
*   Pinch of salt*

¼ teaspoon cumin
2 tablespoons green chili salsa
*   or chili sauce*

GREEN SALAD

Prepare enough of the following for 6 salads:
A mixture of your favorite salad greens, washed and dried
Garbanzo beans
Green onions, chopped
Croutons, preferably homemade

1. Combine sour cream, mayonnaise, garlic powder, salt, cumin, and chili salsa in a small bowl.

2. Toss dressing with salad greens, garbanzo beans, and onions in a large salad bowl. Garnish with croutons.

GRAPE ALMOND PIE
CRUST

½ cup butter   1 cup all-purpose flour
½ cup toasted almonds,   ¼ cup sugar
   finely chopped

1. Melt butter in skillet over medium heat. Add almonds, flour, and sugar, stirring until golden, dry, and crumbly. Reserve 1/4 cup crust mixture for topping.

2. Press remaining crust mixture into bottom of an 8-inch cake pan. Set aside.

FILLING

1 package lemon gelatin   1 cup sour cream
½ cup sugar   1 cup seedless grapes, halved*
1 cup boiling water   GARNISH

1. Dissolve gelatin and sugar in boiling water in a medium bowl, blending well. Place mixture in refrigerator until it begins to thicken, but is not completely jelled.

2. Whisk sour cream into gelatin mixture.

3. Fold in grapes.

4. Pour filling into prepared pan. Top with reserved crust mixture. Chill until set. Serve pie on dessert plates garnished with grape clusters.

Red Flame seedless grapes are a good choice, since they have a wonderful crunchy texture and add color to the pie.

GARNISH

6 small clusters of grapes,
4-5 grapes per bunch

1 egg white, slightly beaten
Granulated sugar

1. Dip grape clusters into egg white. Roll grapes in sugar to coat. Refrigerate dipped grapes until chilled.

Dinner for Four

Beer Batter Shrimp with Orange Ginger Sauce

Baby Bibb and Watercress Salad with Pistachios
Balsamic Vinaigrette

"Fajitas" Sizzling Skirt Steak

Pico de Gallo

"Killer" Bread

Marquis au Chocolat

WINES:

With the Shrimp—Grgich Hills Chardonnay, 1983

With the "Fajitas"—Charles Krug Cabernet Sauvignon, 1980

Angelo Truisi, General Manager

Matthew di Sabella, Executive Chef

If sheer numbers are an indication of success or popularity, the Swan Court Cafe has won over the hearts and stomachs of Napa. Located in the courtyard of the newly opened Embassy Suites Hotel, Swan Court Cafe serves lunch and dinner from one eclectic menu of diverse foods. It allows diners to pick and choose from fun foods like "Killer" Bread, savory BBQ Baby Back Ribs, sizzling Fajitas served with tortillas and salsa, Fried Herb Cheese, thick Beer Batter Onion Rings, Shots of Oysters, and Miniature Three Cheese Pizzas. More serious diners might select from a variety of fresh fish, or one of the four tender cuts of 21-day aged, Midwestern corn- fed beef that is served with a choice of Bearnaise, Pesto, or Horseradish sauce.

Sweet freaks can indulge in a tempting selection of homemade desserts or "go crazy" at the Chocoholic Emporium, a seemingly endless toppings bar for plain, old ice cream. The Emporium displays a visually pleasing selection of treats that includes crumbled Oreo cookies, Malted Milk Balls, and Heath Bars, to name a few.

Heading up the food service operation for Swan Court Cafe and the entire hotel is Matthew di Sabella, a Culinary Institute graduate with plenty of hands-on experience in large operations like Saga Foods and the Silverado Country Club. Happy as a clam to be back in Napa Valley, Chef di Sabella describes the cuisine as "simple and fresh, that's our motto".

The Swan Court Cafe is spacious, colorful, and cheery. A courtyard effect is achieved with surrounding iron gates, quarry tile floors, and large European umbrellas. Completing the scene is a duck pond that flows through the middle of the restaurant, complete with quacking ducks.

1075 California Boulevard
Napa, California

BEER BATTER SHRIMP WITH ORANGE GINGER SAUCE

12-16 large shrimp
   (buy the largest you can find)
1 tablespoon lemon juice
1 can Heineken beer
1 cup all-purpose flour, sifted
1 tablespoon paprika
   ORANGE-GINGER SAUCE

Pinch of baking powder
Salt to taste
Cooking oil
All-purpose flour,
  for dredging shrimp
Fresh cilantro

1. Clean and deveined shrimp. Cut shrimp down the back, keeping the tail shell attached. Sprinkle shrimp with lemon juice; set aside.

2. Combine beer, flour, paprika, baking powder, and salt in a bowl. Beat mixture with a wire whisk until smooth.

3. Fill a deep fat fryer or 3 to 4 quart heavy saucepan one-half full with cooking oil. Heat fat to 375 degrees.

4. Dip shrimp into flour and shake off excess. Holding shrimp by the tail, dip into beer batter. Allow excess batter to run off and then place into hot oil. Deep fry shrimp for 5 minutes, or until golden brown and crisp. Drain fried shrimp on paper towels. Serve immediately with ORANGE-GINGER SAUCE.

To serve, arrange 3 to 4 shrimp on individual serving plates. Place an orange "shell" onto each plate. Garnish with cilantro.

ORANGE-GINGER SAUCE

¾ cup orange marmalade
4 tablespoons lemon juice
2 tablespoons orange juice
1 tablespoon prepared horseradish
½ teaspoon powdered ginger

½ teaspoon dry English mustard
Pinch of white pepper
Pinch of salt
2 Oranges

1. Combine marmalade, lemon juice, orange juice, horseradish, ginger, mustard, salt, and white pepper in a blender; mix for 15 seconds.

2. Cut oranges in half and hollow out each half. Spoon sauce into "shells".

BABY BIBB AND WATERCRESS SALAD WITH PISTACHIOS
BALSAMIC VINAIGRETTE

4 tablespoons pistachio nuts
2 heads baby Bibb lettuce
8 sprigs of watercress

1 small cucumber, cut into rounds
2 small tomatoes, cut into slices
BALSAMIC VINAIGRETTE

1. Preheat oven to 350 degrees. Toast pistachio nuts in a shallow baking pan for 10 minutes, shaking pan occasionally to prevent burning.

2. Cut heads of lettuce in half and wash well under cold running water. Shake off all excess water and remove core. Gently wash and dry watercress.

3. To serve, place lettuce cut side up on salad plates, leaving the outer green leaves as an underliner. Place alternating slices of tomato and cucumber beside the lettuce. Tuck watercress sprigs into lettuce. Sprinkle with toasted pistachio nuts. Drizzle BALSAMIC VINAIGRETTE lightly over salads.

BALSAMIC VINAIGRETTE

⅓ cup Balsamic vinegar
1 cup salad oil
1 teaspoon dry English mustard
1 teaspoon finely minced garlic

¼ teaspoon finely minced shallots
¼ teaspoon sugar
Pinch of salt
Pinch of white pepper

1. Combine Balsamic vinegar, oil, dry mustard, garlic, shallots, sugar, salt, and white pepper in a blender on medium speed for 1 minute.

SWAN COURT CAFE

"FAJITAS" SIZZLING SKIRT STEAK

1 teaspoon Kosher salt
1 teaspoon cracked black pepper
1 teaspoon paprika
1 teaspoon chili powder
1 teaspoon turmeric
1 teaspoon onion powder
1 teaspoon granulated garlic
1 teaspoon ground cumin
4 6-ounce skirt steaks,
  trimmed of all fat

4 teaspoons lime juice
¼ cup salad oil
2 tablespoons salad oil
1 large onion, thinly sliced
8-12 flour tortillas, warm
1 cup sour cream
8 ounces cheddar cheese, grated
  Guacamole
  PICO DE GALLO SALSA

1. The day before serving "Fajitas", season skirt steaks.

2. Combine Kosher salt, pepper, paprika, chili powder, turmeric, onion powder, garlic, and cumin in a small bowl. Lightly dust skirt steaks on both sides with seasoning mixture. Coat steaks lightly with lime juice, and ¼ cup oil. Cover and marinate overnight.

3. Prepare a hot grill with Mesquite charcoal. (If no grill is available, the steaks maybe cooked under a broiler.) Broil marinated steaks until rare, about 2 to 3 minutes on each side. Slice steaks thinly against the grain of the meat.

4. Toss together 1 tablespoon oil, the sliced steak, and onions in a large sauté pan over high heat for 1 minute.

5. Heat a large iron skillet over medium-high heat. Add 1 tablespoon oil to skillet. Quickly add steak mixture to the hot skillet and rush the sizzling Fajitas to the table. Serve sizzling fajitas immediately from the iron skillet.

6. Serve Fajitas with warm flour tortillas, sour cream, grated cheddar cheese, guacamole, and PICO DE GALLO SALSA. Guests may make individual Fajitas burritos if they wish.

Final preparation of this dish takes only a few minutes, so have all accompaniments to the "Fajitas" ready to serve.

PICO DE GALLO SALSA

1 medium white onion, diced
2 medium ripe tomatoes,
   cored and diced

½ bunch cilantro, chopped
Salt and pepper to taste

1. Combine onion, tomatoes, cilantro, and salt and pepper in a bowl. Let stand several hours before serving.

"KILLER" BREAD

1 small round loaf French bread
¼ cup butter, at room temperature
½ cup Parmesan cheese,
   freshly grated

¼ cup mayonnaise
2 teaspoons finely minced
   garlic

1. Preheat oven to 350 degrees.

2. Split bread in half horizontally. Reserve half for another use.

3. Combine butter and garlic in a small bowl. Spread butter mixture over cut side of bread. Toast bread, unwrapped, for 5 minutes, or until golden. Remove from oven. Turn on broiler.

4. Combine mayonnaise and Parmesan cheese in a small bowl. Spread mayonnaise mixture over cut side of toasted bread. Broil until golden brown. Slice bread and serve immediately.

MARQUIS AU CHOCOLAT

1 cup butter
2 cups semi-sweet chocolate bits
3 eggs
½ cup sugar

¼ cup milk
1 cup whipping cream
Fresh raspberries
Mint leaves

1. Melt butter and chocolate in top of a double boiler over simmering water stirring until smooth. Set aside.

2. Whisk eggs and sugar in a bowl. Scald milk in a small, heavy saucepan. Allow milk to cool slightly. Slowly pour milk into egg mixture, whisking constantly until combined.

3. Whisk egg mixture into melted chocolate over warm water bath. Pour Marquis into a serving bowl; cover and refrigerate overnight.

4. To serve, in a chilled bowl with chilled beaters beat whipping cream until stiff peaks form. Scoop Marquis with a small scoop that has been dipped in water. Place two scoops of Marquis on each dessert plate. Place two scoops of whipped cream on either side of Marquis. Garnish with raspberries and mint leaves.

The flavor of this sinfully delicious chocolate dessert improves with age. It should be prepared a day in advance.

For variation, serve Marquis on top of a pool of strawberry or raspberry purée.

Venturi's

Dinner for Six

Shrimp Venturi

Chicken Escoffier

Baby Limestone Salad

Kona Coffee Crèpes with Strawberry Sauce

WINES:

With the Shrimp—1984 Sterling Sauvignon Blanc

With the Chicken—1983 Chateau Montelena Chardonnay
Alexander Valley

With the Crepe—1985 Folie à Deux Muscat à Deux

Tim Venturi, Sean Barrett, Kathy Mack,
and Victor Manuel de Almeida Lopes
Owners

Tim Venturi, Chef

As residents know and visitors soon discover, after dark in St. Helena offers little else for entertainment than a quiet dinner or movie and an early retirement. That is, until Tim Venturi opened his lively restaurant and nightclub in the Cement Works Shopping Center. With nightly dancing until 2 A.M., live entertainment midweek through the weekend, and live jazz every Sunday afternoon, Tim and his energetic partners have added a new dimension to Napa Valley life.

Venturi's is a two-story building with a spacious, informal dining room that overlooks the nightclub. Lunch and dinner are served daily either indoors or on an airy, covered deck. An eclectic menu offers a wide variety of specialties, from full dinners to a savory selection of tasty appetizers, such as carpaccio, fresh oysters, tempura prawns, nachos, and sashimi.

An energetic young man, Tim Venturi is quite experienced in the food world. He previously operated two restaurant-nightclubs in California and most recently held the position of assistant chef at Meadowood Resort in St. Helena. Tim designed the menu himself, selecting "everything I like". Dinners range from fresh seafoods like sautéed scallops and Hawaiian Ahi to vegetarian pasta to chicken, pheasant and duckling. A savory selection of appetizers is prepared throughout the day and served in the restaurant or nightclub, giving patrons the option of either catching a bite, or lingering over a fine dinner.

So when hunger strikes at midnight or you get a sudden urge to dance, head on over to Venturi's for a little bit of what you're looking for.

3111 North St. Helena Highway
St. Helena

SHRIMP VENTURI

1 ounce clarified butter
1½ pound shrimp,
 (16-20 count)
 cleaned and deveined
2 ounces Tequila
½ pound unsalted butter
1 tablespoon fresh garlic,
 finely minced

1 teaspoon lemon juice
2 tablespoons parsley,
 finely chopped
6 lemon wedges
6 lime wedges

1. Add the clarified butter to a large skillet and place it over medium high heat.

2. Just before the skillet comes to the smoking stage add the shrimp all at once.*
   Sauté for two minutes, moving the skillet at all times.

3. Pour tequila over the shrimp. Tequila will flame for about 30 seconds.

4. When flame subsides, add the unsalted butter, garlic and lemon juice. Reduce
   heat to low and reduce the sauce for approximately two minutes.

5. Divide shrimp among six plates. Garnish each plate with a sprinkle of chopped
   parsley and a lemon and lime wedge.

6. Serve with crusty French bread.

*The key to sautéed food is preparing a hot skillet. Otherwise, the butter is
absorbed into the item being cooked.

CHICKEN ESCOFFIER

4 ounces clarified butter
6 8-ounce chicken breasts,
   boned and skinned
   Salt and pepper
4 ounces brandy
½ pound unsalted butter

2 tablespoons shallots,
   finely minced
¾ pound fresh mushrooms,
   sliced
1 pint whipping cream

1. Preheat oven to 350 degrees.

2. Add clarified butter to a large ovenproof skillet. Place over high heat.

3. Meanwhile, season chicken breasts with salt and pepper. When skillet is hot, reduce heat to medium, add breasts and sauté for three to four minutes per side. Place skillet into oven for ten minutes.

4. Remove from oven and place on medium heat. Add brandy, allow to flame. When flames subside reduce heat to low and add butter, moving skillet while butter melts.

5. Remove breasts from skillet. Add shallots and sauté for 30 seconds. Add mushrooms and sauté for another 3 minutes.

6. Add cream to skillet and reduce for 3 or 4 minutes until a creamy consistency is achieved. Taste for seasoning.

7. Add chicken back to pan to glaze it with the sauce for 30 seconds. Remove from heat and arrange on serving plates. Cover with sauce.

8. Serve with oven roasted potatoes and your favorite seasonal vegetable.

BABY LIMESTONE SALAD

6 heads baby limestone lettuce
¼ cup pine nuts
¼ cup fresh lemon juice
   pinch of salt
   pinch of black pepper
   pinch of basil
   pinch of thyme

½ teaspoon garlic,
   finely minced
1 tablespoon fresh chives,
   finely chopped
½ cup olive oil
½ red bell pepper,
   julienned

1. Preheat oven to 350 degrees.

2. Wash and dry lettuce. Split each head down the center and place on salad plates.

3. Place pine nuts on a shallow baking sheet and toast them in the oven for 7 minutes or until golden brown.

4. Combine lemon juice, salt, pepper, basil, thyme, garlic, chives and olive oil in a container with a lid. Shake well.

5. Pour approximately 3 tablespoons of the vinaigrette over each salad. Sprinkle toasted pine nuts over.

6. Garnish with julienned strips of red pepper.

KONA COFFEE CREPES WITH STRAWBERRY SAUCE

1 cup all purpose flour
½ plus 2 tablespoons water
½ cup milk
3 large eggs
2 tablespoons unsalted butter
   melted and cooled
½ teaspoon salt

1 ounce melted unsalted butter,
   for brushing inside of pan
2 pints Kona coffee ice cream,
   (or your favorite coffee ice cream)
1 pint fresh ripe strawberries,
   washed and hulled
1 ounce Sambuca di Romano coffee
   liqueur

CREPE BATTER

1. In a blender or food processor blend the flour, water, milk, eggs, 2 tablespoons butter and salt for 5 seconds. Turn off motor and scrape down the sides with a spatula. Blend another 20 seconds.

2. Transfer batter to a bowl and let it stand, covered, for an hour. Crepe batter may be made a day in advance and kept covered and chilled.

3. Heat a crepe pan or a 5 or 6 inch nonstick pan over medium heat. Brush pan lightly with remaining butter and allow to heat until hot but not smoking.

4. Remove pan from heat. Gently stir crepe batter. Half fill a ¼ cup measure with batter and pour into pan. Tilt and rotate pan quickly to cover bottom with a thin layer of batter. Return pan to heat. Cook until lightly browned, then turn and lightly brown the other side. Transfer crepe to a plate.

5. Make crepes in same manner, using remaining batter. Crepes may be made in advance, stacked, wrapped in plastic wrap, and chilled for up to 3 days or frozen. Makes about 20 crepes.

6. Lay crepes out on a flat work surface. Using a knife, spread about 3 ounce of ice cream over each crepe. Roll up and place in freezer until 10 or 15 minutes prior to serving.

STRAWBERRY SAUCE

1. In a blender or food processor, purée all but six of the strawberries. Reserve these 6 for garnish. Put purée through a sieve to remove seeds.

2. Blend Sambucca di Romano into the purée.

3. Chill sauce in a covered container until ready to use.

To serve, ladle 1 ounce of Strawberry sauce on each dessert plate. Top with a rolled crepe. Garnish with a fresh strawberry.

Appetizers

Andouille Pig Tails *(Bombard's)* .. 25

Andouille Pig Tails Crust
(Bombard's) 32

Beer Batter Shrimp With Orange
Ginger Sauce *(Swan Court)* ...175

Cornmeal Pancake With Caviar and
Crème Fraîche *(Mustards)* 137

Fresh Cured Salmon with Lemon-
Thyme Vinaigrette
(Meadowood) 109

Fresh Duck Foie Gras In A Salad of
Local Greens *(Cafe Oriental)* .. 45

Fricassée of Wild Mushrooms
(Auberge du Soleil) 5

Fried Calamari with Mama Nina's
Special Sauce *(Mama Nina's)* .. 99

Les Escargots Aux Champignons
Sauvages *(La Belle Hélène)* 15

Monkfish with Red Bell Pepper Sauce
(Mt. View) 129

Shrimp Venturi *(Venturi's)* 183

Smoked Salmon Mousse With Black
Caviar *(Calistoga Inn)* 53

Steamed Mussels with Ginger,
Shiitake Mushrooms and Chinese
Fermented Black Beans
(Silverado) 159

Warm Salad of Sweetbreads and
Mushrooms *(French
Laundry)* 89

Breads

"Killer" Bread *(Swan Court)* 178

Skillet Cracklin' Cornbread
(Bombard's) 29

Desserts & Dessert Accents

Almond Pear Tart *(Mt. View)* ... 133

Bread Pudding with Bourbon Sauce
(D.D. Kay's) 66

Chocolate Decadence Cake *(Country
Club)* 155

Chocolate Macadamia and Caramel
Tarte *(Silverado)* 163

Crème Brûlée *(Miramonte)* 124

Frangipan Torte
(Meadowood)................. 114

Frozen Blackberry Souffle *(Calistoga
Inn)* 56

Grape Almond Pie *(Spring
St.)* 170

Grapefruit And Oranges With
Bourbon Creme *(Bombard's)* ...31

Kona Coffee Crepes With Strawberry
Sauce *(Venturi's)* 186

La Crème Glacée Aux Framboises
Dan Son Sac En Chocolat
(Domaine Chandon) 85

Marquis Au Chocolat *(Swan
Court)* 179

Pashka *(St. George)* 149

Passion Fruit Cheese Cake *(Auberge
du Soleil)* 10

Pecan Pie *(Bombard's)* 32

Pecan Pie Crust *(Bombard's)* 32

Poached Pears with Creme Anglaise
(La Belle Hélène) 18

Rhubarb Shortcake *(French
Laundry)* 93

Strawberries Martine *(La
Boucane)* 40

The Diner's Famous Flan
(*Diner*) 77
Torta Della Nonna-Grandmother's
Cake (*Mama Nina's*) 104
Vanilla Bavarois With Fraises Des
Bois (*Cafe Oriental*) 49
Vanilla Ice Cream (*Mustards*) ... 143

Entrées

Aunt Polly's Lamb Shanks (*French
Laundry*) 91
Bakery Lane Frittata (*Spring
St.*) 168
Braised Sea Bass With Saffron and
Mussels (*Calistoga Inn*) 55
Chicken Escoffier (*Venturi's*) ... 184
"Fajitas" Sizzling Skirt Steak (*Swan
Court*) 177
File Gumbo:Seafood, Fish, Sausage,
Chicken and Ham
(*Bombard's*) 27
Fricassée Of Fresh Pheasant In Cain's
Cabernet Jelly (*La Belle
Hélène*) 16
Grilled Fresh Pork With Roasted
Tomato and Toasted Chili Peppers
(*Silverado*) 160
Grilled Rabbit With Tomato Chipotle
Salsa and Black Beans
(*Mustards*) 138
Grilled Squab With Spinach And
Beurre Blanc (*Cafe Oriental*) ... 48
Grilled Tuna With Sunshine Salsa
(*Diner*) 73
L'Agneau Au Yogurt Dans La Sauce
Au Cabernet (*Miramonte*) 122
Lamb Chops Calabrian (*Mama
Nina's*) 102

LeMagret De Canard Au Cabernet
Avec Les Chanterelles (*Domaine
Chandon*) 83
Les Saint Jacques Marinées Aux
Deux Citrons Et Coriandre
(*Domaine Chandon*) 82
Linguine Roberta (*D.D. Kay's*) 61
Loin of Milk-Fed Veal With Pancetta
And Basil Port Wine and Orange
Sauce (*Meadowood*) 112
Maple Leaf Duck with Blueberry
Sauce (*D.D. Kay's*) 63
Medallions Of Veal And Prawns
(*Country Club*) 154
Papillôte Of California King Salmon
And Elephant Garlic (*Cafe
Oriental*) 46
Partridge with Two Purées and Purple
Basil Fumé (*Auberge du
Soleil*) 7
Pollo San Giorgio (*St.
George*) 148
Roast Sirloin Strip Of Beef With
Green Peppercorn Sauce (*Mt.
View*) 131
Salmon Poached With Champagne
Sauce (*La Boucane*) 39
Steamed Blue Maine Mussels (*D.D.
Kay's*) 62

Pasta and Rice

Aegean Pasta (*St. George*) 147
Bucatini All'Amatriciana (*Mama
Nina's*) 101
Parslied Rice (*Diner*) 74
Rice (*Bombard's*) 30

Pineapple Sorbet *(Mt. View)* 130

Salads and Salad Dressings

Arrugula Salad with Raspberry
  vinaigrette *(D.D. Kay's)* 65
Baby Bibb And Watercress Salad
  With Pistachios *(Swan
  Court)* 176
Baby Limestone Salad
  (Venturi's) 185
Balsamic Vinaigrette *(Swan
  Court)* 176
Crème Fraîche *(Diner)* 72
Crème Fraîche *(Mustards)* 138
Fresh Tomato and Corn Salad with
  Basil and Garlic *(Diner)* 71
Garden Tomato Salad
  (Mustards) 142
Green Salad With Cumin Dressing
  (Spring St.) 169
Macedoine California *(La
  Boucane)* 37
Mediterranean Spinach Salad *(St.
  George)* 147
Mixed Green Salad with Creamy
  Basil Dressing *(Mama
  Nina's)* 100
Simple Green Salad *(French
  Laundry)* 92
Sooey Salad *(Bombard's)* 26
Spring Salad *(Auberge du Soleil)* .. 9
Vinaigrette *(Diner)* 71
Warm Scallops With Young Greens
  (Silverado) 162
Wilted Wisconsin Duck Salad
  (Country Club) 153

Sorbets

Soups

Cabbage Ham Soup *(Spring
  St.)* 167
Cream of Mushroom Soup A La
  Jacques *(La Boucane)* 38
La Crème De Tomates En Croute
  (Domaine Chandon) 81
Red Bell Pepper and Tomato Soup
  (Calistoga Inn) 54
Sopa de Chile Verde *(Diner)* 72
Sorrel Soup *(French Laundry)* ... 90
Soupe De Poisson
  (Miramonte) 120
Wild Mushroom and Ginger Soup
  With Chervil Leaves
  (Meadowood) 111

Vegetables and Side Dishes

Aubergine Chinoise A La Provencale
  (Miramonte) 119
Black Beans *(Mustards)* 140
Grilled Vegetables with Herb Butter
  (Diner) 75
Red Beans *(Bombard's)* 30

DINING IN-WITH THE GREAT CHEFS

A Collection of Gourmet Recipes from the Finest Chefs in the Country

- ☐ Dining In–Baltimore $7.95
- ☐ Dining In–Boston (Revised) 8.95
- ☐ Dining In–Chicago, Vol. III 8.95
- ☐ Dining In–Cleveland 8.95
- ☐ Dining In–Dallas (Revised) 8.95
- ☐ Dining In–Denver 7.95
- ☐ Dining In–Hampton Roads 8.95
- ☐ Dining In–Hawaii 7.95
- ☐ Dining In–Houston, Vol. II 7.95
- ☐ Dining In–Kansas City (Revised) 7.95
- ☐ Dining In–Los Angeles (Revised) 8.95
- ☐ Dining In–Manhattan 8.95
- ☐ Dining In–Miami 8.95
- ☐ Dining In–Milwaukee 7.95
- ☐ Dining In–Minneapolis/St. Paul, Vol. II . . . 8.95
- ☐ Dining In–Monterey Peninsula 7.95
- ☐ Dining In–Napa Valley 8.95
- ☐ Dining In–New Orleans 8.95
- ☐ Dining In–Philadelphia 8.95
- ☐ Dining In–Phoenix 8.95
- ☐ Dining In–Pittsburgh (Revised) 7.95
- ☐ Dining In–Portland 7.95
- ☐ Dining In–St. Louis 7.95
- ☐ Dining In–Salt Lake City 8.95
- ☐ Dining In–San Francisco, Vol II 7.95
- ☐ Dining In–Seattle 8.95
- ☐ Dining In–Sun Valley 7.95
- ☐ Dining In–Toronto 7.95
- ☐ Dining In–Vancouver, B.C. 8.95
- ☐ Dining In–Washington, D.C. 8.95

THE EPICURES

Menu Guides to the Better Restaurants in Each City . . .
New, updated Epicures due out Fall '86

- ☐ Baltimore Epicure $7.95
- ☐ Boston Epicure 7.95
- ☐ Chicago Epicure 7.95
- ☐ Dallas Epicure 7.95
- ☐ Denver Epicure 7.95
- ☐ Detroit Epicure 7.95
- ☐ Honolulu Epicure 7.95
- ☐ Houston Epicure 7.95
- ☐ Kansas City Epicure 7.95
- ☐ Los Angeles Epicure 7.95
- ☐ Manhattan Epicure $7.95
- ☐ Miami Epicure 7.95
- ☐ Minneapolis/St. Paul Epicure 7.95
- ☐ New Orleans Epicure 7.95
- ☐ San Diego Epicure 7.95
- ☐ San Francisco Epicure 7.95
- ☐ Seattle Epicure 7.95
- ☐ St. Louis Epicure 7.95
- ☐ Washington D.C. Epicure 7.95
- ☐ The National Epicure 11.95

TO ORDER, SEND LIST PRICE PLUS $1 POSTAGE AND HANDLING FOR EACH BOOK

☐ Check (✔) here if you would like to have a different Dining In–Cookbook sent to you once a month. Payable by MasterCard or VISA. Returnable if not satisfied.

Simply fill out the order form or call . . .

1-800-548-7766

BILL TO:

Name _____

Address _____

City_____ State _____ Zip_____

PEANUT BUTTER PUBLISHING
911 Western Avenue #401
Seattle, Wa. 98104
(206) 628-6200

SHIP TO:

Name _____

Address _____

City _____ State _____ Zip _____

☐ Payment enclosed   ☐ Charge

Visa #_____Exp.____

MasterCard # _____Exp.____

Signature:_____